THE
BIBLE OF TO-DAY

THE
BIBLE OF TO-DAY

by the

REV. ALBAN BLAKISTON, M.A.

Cambridge:
at the University Press
1914

CAMBRIDGE
UNIVERSITY PRESS

University Printing House, Cambridge CB2 8BS, United Kingdom

Cambridge University Press is part of the University of Cambridge.

It furthers the University's mission by disseminating knowledge in the pursuit of education, learning and research at the highest international levels of excellence.

www.cambridge.org
Information on this title: www.cambridge.org/9781316620007

© Cambridge University Press 1914

First published 1914
First paperback edition 2016

A catalogue record for this publication is available from the British Library

ISBN 978-1-316-62000-7 Paperback

PREFACE

THE attempt is made, in the following pages, to introduce the student of the Bible to what is known as the historical, or critical, method of studying the Scriptures and investigating their messages. The volume does not aim at supplying introductions to the separate books. Such an aim, if it were in any way to be satisfied, would require a volume of far greater compass than this. The purpose is, rather, to present to the reader the point of view which is responsible for applying the historical method of treatment to the sacred pages, and to envisage the 'atmosphere,' intellectual and religious, which is the outcome of that treatment. To this end, it has appeared desirable to give a brief survey of the whole field of Biblical study, which should be in some measure preliminary to the special introductions. In an introductory chapter the question of Inspiration is briefly discussed. The second chapter deals with the Text of the Old Testament, and seeks to trace, in outline, the history of its different writings ; endeavouring to grasp, on the one hand, what were the causes which determined their form and contents ; and, on the other hand, how they came to be combined in a single volume to which a

peculiar sanctity was attached. The third chapter deals
with the New Testament upon similar lines. And, in
the last chapter, it is attempted to show what were
the influences which contributed to the development of
the Jewish and Christian religions, in so far as the books
of the Old and New Testaments exhibit this sort of
dependence. Incidentally a great many other subjects
are touched upon.

In order to secure for the book a readable form and
style, it was felt that its pages should not be over-loaded
with detailed information ; but a fairly comprehensive
list of books appended to each chapter will, it is hoped,
assist the reader who may desire a fuller acquaintance
with the matters under discussion. There is also added,
as an appendix, a list of writings, canonical and extra-
canonical, arranged (often quite provisionally) in chronological order ; in the hope that the student may thus be
aided to grasp the historical setting of the various books,
and their relation to the Jewish and Christian literatures
as a whole.

The book lays claim to no sort of originality, but
is dependent throughout upon the labours of well-known
scholars. The author's sense of indebtedness is, in some
measure, expressed by the lists of books which follow
upon each chapter. On the other hand it has frequently
been necessary to select, by the exercise of individual
judgment, and present to the reader, one amongst many

rival opinions; and it is hoped that, in such places, a tone of dogmatism has been successfully avoided.

It remains for the author to tender his sincere thanks to Mr F. W. Sanderson, Headmaster of Oundle School, and to the Rev. S. C. Parmiter of Uppingham School, who have read the MS. in part, for much valuable criticism and advice; also to the Publishers' Reader for the detection of several errors and blemishes. He would also express his gratitude to Mr W. E. Weber, at whose instance the work was undertaken, for an unfailing kindness in the course of its production, which has been a great source of encouragement.

A. B.

30th Jan. 1914

TABLE OF CONTENTS

CHAPTER I

THE INSPIRATION OF SCRIPTURE AND THE METHOD OF BIBLICAL STUDY

CHAPTER II

THE TEXT, LITERATURE AND CANON OF THE OLD TESTAMENT

CHAPTER III

THE TEXT, CANON AND LITERATURE OF THE NEW TESTAMENT

CHAPTER IV

THE RELIGIOUS AFFINITIES OF JUDAISM AND CHRISTIANITY

CONTENTS

CHAPTER I

THE INSPIRATION OF SCRIPTURE AND THE METHOD OF BIBLICAL STUDY

1. DURING the last fifty years, more or less, a great change has come upon the manner in which Christians regard and study their Bible. In one sense, perhaps, the volume of Scripture is rather less to us at the present day than it was to our fathers; but in every other sense it is a great deal more. If our fathers treated the Bible as the Mohammedans treat their Koran, or as the Jewish Rabbis in the early Christian centuries undoubtedly treated our Old Testament; if, that is, they regarded it as a literally inspired book, in the composition of which the human writer was a mere machine, who wrote word for word what God dictated: then the Bible is less to us than it was to them. But if we have learnt how God actually worked through His human instruments; if we have come to see what inspiration really implied; if we are now able to trace the steps by which, under God's guidance, the Bible very gradually grew to be the volume we have in our hands: then our gain is very great indeed. For, not only has our understanding of its

Change in our treatment of the Bible.

messages vastly increased, but the Scriptures themselves are found to be a much more wonderful volume than our fathers ever supposed. Just as God revealed Himself in and through our own nature, when He took upon Him our flesh and became Man; so His Word, in all ages, came into the world under the conditions of human life, when He spoke to men through His prophets and apostles. The Bible is not a mechanical composition, but a very human document.

2. Some fifty years ago, more or less, the great majority of Christians supposed that our universe and all that it contains was created, in the form in which we now know it, by the spoken word of God, in a very short space of time some six thousand years ago. But Science has compelled us to alter our opinion. And what is Science but the wisdom man has learnt by the use of God's great gift of reason, which he has very properly directed to the studying and understanding of God's work in Nature? We now know that the universe in which we live, including man himself, is the result of a process of development, generally called evolution, which has extended, in its slow operations, through untold myriads of years, and which is to be attributed to the action, and inter-action, of certain dimly understood forces, which are themselves the material expression of God's will. Science does not exclude God from His universe; but she teaches that God's method of working has been very different from what we had imagined. And knowing now how He actually has worked, and is working, the universe has become to us a far more marvellous and majestic thing than we had previously dreamed of.

The history of the composition of the Bible is not

Similar to change in way of regarding Nature.

very different from that of the formation of our universe. We can trace the same process of evolution, spread over a long period of time; we can mark the same action and inter-action of little understood forces, which express the very mind of God. For the Bible has come into being only after the lapse of many hundreds of years, during which it was subject to many kinds of change and all the vicissitudes of fortune; and during which, also, God's mind and will were working their way slowly upwards in the intelligence and conscience of His servants; until, very gradually, and by almost imperceptible steps, His word attained to a clearer expression, and, through His human agents and under human conditions, He was able to reveal Himself fully to His children. When we understand this, God's Book, or rather His Library of Books, becomes to us not a whit less wonderful and beautiful than that other open Book of God, Nature herself.

3. The change which has recently transpired, then, rather lifts the Bible to a higher place in our esteem, than depresses it. For it does not affect the inspiration and religious value of Scripture, except to enhance them in our regard. What it has done has been to affect very deeply our method of study and interpretation, as we have come to grasp more intelligently the means God has chosen to reveal Himself to us. The new method is that known as 'historical.' It is not a method invented by captious critics for the purpose of discrediting the Bible; but it is a method forged by scholars in other fields of research, and now first applied to the Bible, both because of the valuable results which have been derived from it elsewhere, and because it was felt that the Bible could no

The change affects, not inspiration, but method of study.

longer stand alone, isolated from the whole region of learned research. Now the application of this method, as we shall see, involves treating the Bible as we should treat any other very ancient piece of literature. We may even go further and say that, in proportion as we value the Bible above every other literature, so our study of it will be more rigorous and exact and candid. But this readiness to submit our Sacred Writings to what is called criticism need not shock our sense of reverence. For it is largely in that way that we discover how different the Bible is from every other literature the world has ever seen. The more light we are able to shed upon its pages, from every possible point of view, only brings into greater prominence the fact, which we hold so dear, that the Bible is unlike every other book.

4. That being so, it obviously demands of us a very special reverence in our handling of it.

Great reverence needed in study of Scripture.

The Christian student can never afford to forget, what is indeed patent in every page of Scripture, that in it we possess the great and final authority in all spiritual matters, the inspired guide to religious feeling and thought, the Divine Truth which reveals to us the Way by which we may obtain Eternal Life, the supreme educator of character and the standard of human morality and righteousness; and, indeed, a great deal more, as all ages of Christian men and women have realised in their own use and experience of it. In short, we shall ever remember that in these days, when it is no longer possible or desirable to confine ourselves to the study of one book, the Bible is still *par excellence the* book; truly human in the manner in which it has come into existence; but, even because of that, for its inestimable and inexhaustible worth, truly Divine.

5. This twofold aspect of the Scriptures, the Divine
Meaning of   spirit borne by the human form, the trea-
Inspiration.   sure which resides in the earthly vessels,
leads us on to ask more particularly what Inspiration is,
and to discover how it should affect our reading of the
Bible. The fact of Inspiration is of very great importance from the religious point of view, but it is one
of those things which are exceedingly difficult to define,
and which, happily, the Christian Church has not ventured to define. We may, and do, recognise, in our
reading of them, that certain books are inspired; and we
may feel the full force of that inspiration: but when we
attempt to explain how, and in what direction, the
inspiration operates, the matter is found mysteriously to
elude our mental grasp; so that we can offer no more
than an inadequate description of the process.

In the first place, we ought to realise quite clearly
(i.) Inspiration   that the books of Scripture form the Record
of Revelation.   of a Revelation. That is to say, the fact
of Inspiration is inseparably bound up with that of
Revelation. Bearing this in mind, we should probably
be right in distinguishing three kinds, or degrees, of Inspiration. There is the Inspiration of Revelation. Now
a study of the Bible itself will show us that Revelation is
a communication, by God to man, of the things which
man may legitimately desire to know, which it concerns
him very nearly to know, and which he can never know
by his own unaided understanding. It is a communication of the Truth; the truth about God, His nature, His
purpose in the creation of the world, His will with
regard to man; the truth about man, his sinful nature,
his need of Divine help, his destiny; the truth about
the relations which exist, or should exist, between God

and man; and countless other matters of similar importance.

This communication was made, directly or indirectly, Its gradual progress. to the hearts and consciences of individual men; and, we may add, in some measure to a whole community or society of men, a nation or a church, as such a society came to grasp and recognise the Truth, and to live by it. The revelation was not, indeed, made all at once; but, rather, was it a long process of education. It came in various portions and at different times, as men were capable of receiving it. In the beginning it was very simple, very elementary, very crude; and, naturally, it was almost swamped by the magical superstitions, intellectual errors, and immoral customs, with which it was mingled in those primitive times. But gradually it emerged from that early darkness into daylight, as its force began to be felt, and people responded to its influence, and ignorance was purged away. It expanded in the range of its teaching, it grew to be fuller and deeper and richer, it became more spiritual. And even now our Biblical studies enable us to follow, in part, this slow development of revelation.

Then, with the appearance of our Lord Jesus Christ, Culminating in our Lord. God suddenly opened, upon that Divinely-Human understanding, the full flood of His personal manifestation of Himself to the human race. Through Him, He declared all that man can ever know of the great realities which lie behind our life here on earth.

And yet, though God's Revelation reached its highest Continued through the Apostles. and final limit in Jesus Christ, the process of communication did not altogether cease at that point. For now there arose a succession of apostolic men, and a society which came to be known as the Christian Church, to whom God's Holy Spirit made known the full meaning of what had been shown to man in the Incarnate Son of God. The supremest disclosure of all needed its authoritative interpretation. And this process of interpretation was also gradual, not being completed all at once.

Nor, even, can we arbitrarily close the period of revelation with the inspired writings of the New Testament. For, in a secondary sense, God reveals Himself anew, in all ages, to every devout student of His written Word; unfolding to each the hidden mysteries of the unique revelation made in Christ Jesus, and disclosing yet further wisdom in a book whose meaning is inexhaustible, and which the world will never outgrow.

(ii.) Inspiration of the reader.

Thus we discern one, or perhaps two forms of Inspiration; the inspiration of the individual to whom the revelation is made; and the inspiration of him who would receive and understand that revelation. And the experience of the latter verifies the truth of the former.

But there is yet another form of Inspiration, which more directly concerns us here; and that is the inspiration of the various writers, compilers, and editors of the books which were not put into literary form by the actual recipient of revelation; and, we may add, the inspiration of the guardians and trustees of the Sacred Writings through the ages. We may, if we please, identify this kind of inspiration with that of those whom God has so gifted that they are able to appreciate and understand the revelation He has accorded them, through the mouths of others. And yet there is a difference.

(iii.) Inspiration of selection, recording, and transmission.

When we study the Bible we actually possess, in the light of the very curious and chequered history through which those records of revelation have passed, we cannot fail to realise that the records themselves, the manifold processes which have given them to us, and their transmission from generation to generation, must possess something of the qualities of the original revelation. If we admit, as we do, that, in the Bible, God Himself speaks to us by means of the inspired utterances and experiences of His chosen servants; then are we bound to acknowledge that the men who collected and wrote and preserved these things for us must also have been, in their measure, inspired by God. In other words, God's hand is to be seen not in the initial act only, but in the continuous process.

We may think of the long period of time during which much of what we now possess was handed down by word of mouth, and was thus dependent upon the faithfulness of human memory; we may think of the arduous winnowing of social laws and customs, until their moral fruitfulness came to stamp them with the marks of Divine approval and sanction; we may think of the gradual purification of old-world legends and allegories, until they assumed a form capable of expressing the profoundest religious truth; we may think of the careful process of selection, in the course of which all that was, from a religious point of view, worthless or irrelevant was cast aside, and only that was chosen which appeared to be instinct with Divine teaching; we may think of the laborious care which was bestowed upon the venerable writings, preserving them from the contamination of irreverent hands, and handing them down, pure and intact, to generations to come; and we may think of the way in which these books survived, almost miraculously, the long lapse of time, the apathy of men, the fatalities of chance, and the wanton hand of the fanatical persecutor. And, bearing these things in mind, we may then ask whether the discernment, appreciation and knowledge, the diligence, awe and love, of so many successive generations, in a race gifted to a peculiar degree with the genius for religion, were not on a similar footing with the inspiration of the original recipients of God's revelation. And the answer can only be in the affirmative.

6. It is worth while to pause here to consider whether the above statement requires to be qualified in certain respects. It may, for instance, be asked whether, in affirming the inspiration of the Scriptures we thereby deny to inspiration a wider latitude than the Canons of the Old and New Testaments. Or it may be objected that we can hardly be expected to affirm inspiration in the same sense of books so dissimilar in character and value as Leviticus or Chronicles and Isaiah or the Fourth Gospel. Or, again, it may be asked whether there has been no religious progress within the Christian Church since the first century; and if so, whether that does not prove that there is no finality about the revelation recorded in the inspired writings. We must endeavour to meet these questions fairly but briefly.

Possible objections to this statement.

In the following chapters we shall have occasion to notice that God's revelation to man was not confined to a particular people (cp. Acts xiv. 17), and that the Jewish faith was, to some extent, the product of influences which reached the people from external sources. The example of Balaam is a proof that this conception of the mode of revelation

(i.) Inspiration wider than Scripture.

was not foreign to the Hebrew mind. We gather that the prophet was always held to be the medium or channel of the communication of the Divine mind to men ; our Lord Himself is spoken of as the Prophet in connection with the unique revelation He came to bring. What was the nature of the prophetic character or temperament is a problem which concerns the psychology of religion ; but it is necessary for us to observe that though the institution of the prophet was destined to play a predominant part in the development of the religion of the Old Testament, and though it appeared again in the early history of the Christian Church, nevertheless it was not confined to the Jewish people. All the peoples of antiquity with whom the Hebrews came in contact had their prophets or seers, whose influence was, so far as we can gather, often for good; and there is no reason why we should deny that these men may frequently have been inspired, or that God spoke to humanity through them. Our reverence for the Bible does not constrain us to depreciate the real religious value of the work of a Zoroaster or a Plato ; and certain early Christian writers were quick to perceive this fact.

On the other hand there is a finality about the (ii.) Scriptural revelation of Scripture which the wider revelation nevertheless view of inspiration does not touch. It is final. possible that our Hebrew writings are only a fragment of a larger religious literature, much of which has been lost. It is not probable, however, in view of what we know of the habits of the Scribes, that anything of unique or striking value has disappeared with the ravages of time. But even should it be the case that some writings of great importance have vanished, this would not of necessity diminish from the whole of revelation. So keenly alive were the prophetic and scribal schools in all ages to the moral and spiritual worth of religious truth, with such a high responsibility did they regard their guardianship of the inspired utterances of holy men, that it is exceedingly unlikely that anything of really vital moment should have been lost. The first statement of a truth may have been superseded, its original form may have given place to a different embodiment or expression; but it would not have disappeared unrecognised. It is, therefore, practically certain that in the Hebrew writings we have the highest and most complete account of the truth as it was revealed to the Jewish people. But there was nothing of finality about that. Judaic religion raises more questions than it can answer. In Jesus Christ, as we believe, the summit of revelation was reached; and if the summit, then the final point. There have doubtless been many prophets in all ages of the Christian Church, prophets who have truly declared the mind of God to their own generation. It may be that we do not lack these prophets in our own times. But it may fairly be asked whether any one of them has contributed anything new to the sum of Divine revelation, and whether we can regard any of their works as inspired in the first degree. It will probably be answered that where they have been most forceful they have but enunciated afresh the truth as it is in Christ. Doubtless they have searched and brought to light much that had remained hidden in the Gospel message; they have analysed and interpreted it afresh, and displayed the richness of the revelation in its application to life; but they have added nothing to the original deposit of truth. Theirs has been the task to which, as it seems, the Christian prophet is appointed;

not to reveal new things, but to expound the old truths
in new ways, and thus to make them live to the conscience
of every successive generation. Thus the Scriptures
remain the record of a revelation which is final, the fulness
of truth for all time.

There is, undoubtedly, a more and a less in the
matter of inspiration. All the writings in
the Bible do not stand upon the same level.
This, the analogy of the arts perhaps would
lead us to expect, and it is proved by our own religious
sense. Moreover, the degree of inspiration may be said
to be suited to the material with which the writer was
concerned. Bare chronicles and legal codes do not
demand the same consummate religious genius as goes
to the production of a moral discourse, an apocalyptic
vision, or a penitential psalm. Nor is it to be expected
that a single writer will always live upon the same plane
of sublime discernment. Further, we may be tempted
to wish that certain writings had obtained a place in the
Old Testament which are relegated to the Apocrypha,
and conversely we may wish away a great deal which
cannot be said to possess any direct religious interest.
A book like Wisdom, we may feel, is at least on the
same level of inspiration as Proverbs; and, though we
would not willingly part with it, we may be inclined to
wonder at the inclusion of so sceptical a work as
Ecclesiastes. But, after all, the Canon of the Old Testament is not infallible. It grew, undoubtedly, under the
inspiration of the Divine guidance; but it was, from the
human side, largely controlled by circumstance; and it
was, as we may say, purely accidental that certain late
books did not obtain an entrance to it. Thus it does
not derogate from the supreme value of the Hebrew

(iii.) Different levels of Inspiration.

Scriptures to acknowledge that their Canon does not in strictness, and with precision, mark the limits of inspiration.

7. Now, if the Bible is pre-eminently an inspired

The contents of an inspired Book will be religious; volume, and if God's method of inspiration has been such as we have indicated, then it is necessary for us, before we go further,

to enquire what we should naturally and reasonably expect to find in a Book of this kind. And the answer is easily forthcoming, and is quite clear. We shall expect to find in it a store-house of religious truth; we shall look for the unmistakable Divine teaching about the things which most nearly concern us men in the moral and religious conduct of our present life; and we shall hope to discover how that may be made a basis for a life to come.

We misconceive the purpose of a Book of this

other than religious truth not to be looked for. character, if we suppose that we should go to the Bible to learn all that man can know of the other concerns of life. God has not

chosen to reveal to us what we are able to learn for ourselves about the world in which we live. On the contrary, He has chosen to endow us with the necessary intellectual equipment, by the use of which He intends us to master and command all the other fields of knowledge. But religious truth is a matter of revelation, simply because we cannot arrive at it by the use of our ordinary faculties; and it is with religious truth that the Bible is concerned. The science, or history, or philosophy of the Scriptures, belongs to the times in which the books respectively were written; they partake of the degree of knowledge, or ignorance, which was common to the age of the writers. Even the religious truth imparted in the

Bible has filtered through the minds of the inspired
men, and has been coloured, in their minds, by the
mental outlook which was their own. That this is so
may be made clear by illustration. A great deal of
what we treat as the pictorial or metaphorical language
of poetry would certainly have been, to the Old Testament
writers, the literal expression of fact. Take, for instance,
the crude conception of God as a sort of magnified
earthly monarch, exalted upon a throne above the world
He has made, just out of view, and coming down from
time to time to visit His people, whether upon a
mountain-top, or in His temple. The religious truth
conveyed by this is undoubtedly that of Acts xvii. (24),
27, 28; cp. John iv. 23, 24; but that truth is conditioned
by current ideas. Or we may notice the ascription to
God of the ordinary human feelings and passions, such
as jealousy; cp. Deut. iv. 24 (cp. 2 Cor. xi. 2, which we
may perhaps paraphrase, 'I am jealous over you with
a jealousy which God must be feeling'); which no doubt
expresses the truth that God's love demands that men
shall love Him, since that way lies human salvation.
And again; when Jesus is called, in the Fourth Gospel,
'the Word,' to describe what He was before the In-
carnation, use is being made of a more or less technical
term of current philosophy; and this too is an illustration
of how the Truth which was revealed to men was,
in different measure, coloured by their own previous
ideas.

Now, all of this is the human factor which enshrines
the Divine; and, to a great extent, it accounts for the
extraordinary human appeal which meets us in every
page of the Book. It is as a scaffolding erected around
the strong tower of religious truth which it is the purpose

of Scripture to manifest. The scaffold is necessary for the erection of the tower; but if we desire to see the tower in all its beauty we must penetrate beyond the scaffold. Therefore it is necessary for us to understand and allow for this human factor, if we are properly to grasp the Divine. And if, in the course of our study, we are obliged to acknowledge this or that piece of history or science or philosophy to be unsound, we shall in no way be disturbed; for the Bible guarantees the trustworthiness of its religious teaching, and nothing more.

8. Further; as we come to study the Bible in an historical way, taking the different books, not only in their chronological order, but also in full view of the circumstances which gave them birth; and as we watch the gradual development of religious knowledge through the ages, from the small unpromising seed to the full-blown flower; we shall not call in question the value of those early religious experiments, which were so often marred by false theology and false morality; for we shall discern, by our historical treatment, a process of revelation which corresponded to men's ripening apprehension of the Divine, and their growing capacity to grasp the Truth; and we shall find in this, both a real source of education for our own un-tutored spiritual needs and powers, and a reflection of the stages along which we ourselves may pass, in the history of our own religious experience.

Value of a gradual re-velation.

9. Thus, if we now ask ourselves whether the Bible is true, we shall be able to return an emphatic affirmative; for it is undoubtedly true in the only sense that is important, in that it presents to our spiritual intelligence a gradual unfolding

The Bible true, and worthy of belief.

of the most vital truth to which man can ever attain, and which he can never exhaust. And if we go on to enquire whether the Bible is to be believed, again the answer will be unhesitating and uncompromising. It is to be believed just in the sense in which we hold it to be true ; it is to be trusted in the sphere in which it claims our allegiance. There are many things in the Bible, no doubt, which are open to correction, because they are not properly *of* the Bible,—vital, that is, to its teaching ; but if we bring to our study of the sacred Book the measure of faith which it requires, then we shall find that our religious experience is deepened and broadened by its holy teaching, and our faith will be completely vindicated.

10. We said, when we began, that of recent years a change has come over our study of the Bible ; and that is true. To-day we find ourselves in a new and invigorating atmosphere. The historical method of study, by which we mean an honest attempt to discover precisely what the Scriptures originally said and meant, brings out every day new and unexpected lines of thought, and other features of interest, the value of which cannot be over-estimated. It seems to stand to reason that the older methods of interpretation,—the allegorical which saw a mystical meaning in everything, or the literal which gave every word an equal value,—could not have been productive of such fruitful results. By the exercise of a certain ingenuity, the unhistorical reader could always read his own ideas and preconceptions into the language of Scripture ; but, as means to discover what God had intended to teach, such methods were foredoomed to failure.

The historical method of interpretation ;

If it be objected that devout souls have, in all ages,
which demands of us long and arduous study. found solace and inspiration in the Bible without the aid of the new learning, the fact cannot be denied. It cannot be too strongly insisted upon that the Bible is God's Book, and that He will, by its means, find His way to the devout soul, however faulty and imperfect the reader's apprehension of the nature of the Book may be. It is one of the standing marvels of this inspired volume, that it can make its home in every heart and mind, whether cultured or the reverse. But that does not affect our contention that a more intelligent way of reading the Bible, which is also equally devout, will give a completer insight into the process and character of God's revelation. In these days the call makes itself heard, and the way is easy, for all to profit by the new method of study. We may remind ourselves that God does not waste His gifts, and that He would never have endowed us with reason if He had meant us to exclude this faculty in the highest of all human exercises, religion itself. We cannot degrade religion by accounting it an easy matter; and the laboriousness of our study of Scripture should not fall far behind the supreme discipline of prayer. Undoubtedly the sacred pages will not yield up to us their hidden treasures of Divine wisdom, unless we apply ourselves to them with long, patient and diligent study.

11. It is obviously true that much of the work
There are the Biblical experts which requires to be done upon the Bible is the task of the devoted scholar and trained expert. Few others can have the time for close and prolonged investigation, even if they possess the requisite talent for such special lines of

scientific research. But he who seeks for information can profit by the results of the experts' labours; particularly in view of the fact that so much is now being given to the public in a popular form. And information of this kind, when it is to be had, should be gladly welcomed by the Biblical student.

Now, since the study of the Bible is, in the hands *whose province is to debate difficult problems,* of scholars, a science, or rather a group of sciences, each of them progressive in character, but many of them still in their infancy; it is only natural to expect that, on many points, we shall look in vain for any unanimity of opinion amongst the experts. In such cases we must await the results with an open mind. The case is the same with Biblical studies as it is with all other fields of knowledge. New interpretations of obscure passages, new historical views, new literary judgments, are constantly being sprung upon us; and the humble student for a while gives place to the learned debate. The combatants join issue, the battle swings to and fro, and, to the outside observer, the dust frequently obscures the main points at issue; until, at length, the superior force of argument gives the victory to one side or the other; and, then, something more is added to the sum of our Biblical knowledge.

Now, it seems fairly clear that, in these days, *and to decide.* scholarship must be our teacher and guide. This does not imply that we should sacrifice our duty of personal study, and take our knowledge at second-hand; but it does mean that we should correct our results by the standard of what is accepted. In all other branches of knowledge there are the recognised authorities, whose guidance we accept, especially when we happen ourselves to be ignorant of their subjects. And so, in Biblical studies also, we have our authorities to whose verdicts we must respectfully bow.

All through the ages of the Christian Church there has been a perennial conflict between con-
*Some au-
thority there
must be;* stituted authority, on the one hand, and the right of private opinion, on the other, in the matter of the interpretation of Scripture. The wholly natural feeling that uninstructed and incompetent private opinion must, on matters of so profound an importance, almost necessarily err, led to a great emphasis being placed on the authority of the Church, as expressed in the decrees of councils, and the writings of Fathers ; an authority which, it was held, could not go far wrong and must not be questioned. And it was in opposition to an arbitrary and despotic suppression of a perfectly legitimate enquiry, that a too exalted opinion was entertained of the right of private judgment. The Church appealed to the guidance of the Holy Spirit as the source of her authority ; but so also did those who disputed her rulings. And if, now, we turn to another sort of authority, it is in the firm belief that we shall find there the leading of God's Spirit.

For, in these days, the kind of ecclesiastical authority
*the authority
of scholarship.* of which we have spoken is not allowed to be the final arbiter on matters of Biblical interpretation. The judgments of Fathers of the Church are not, indeed, to be discarded without being carefully examined and given their full weight; for in them we often have the expression of an opinion which held the field for a long period of time, and which may sometimes go back to a remote antiquity, not far removed from the date of the composition of the inspired writings

themselves. But the principle of authority is based upon God's gift of reason; and it is in the hands of those scholars whose exact studies, and Divinely illumined researches, have given them the responsibility of pronouncing a verdict. Such an authority does not curtail the privilege, or the obligation, of individual study; nor does it close the door to further scientific studies, whose fruits others may sift and weigh. But it does emphasise the folly of those who would make themselves independent of all guidance, and who would claim a right to interpret the Bible as they please;—a claim which often implies, in conformity with their own prejudices. It needs to be said, that the principle of authority is of the utmost importance to all really scientific work, and that it must be maintained.

12. We may now, before we bring the present introductory chapter to a close, briefly review four chief ways of reading the Bible; ways which should be found, if arduous, yet undoubtedly profitable.

Ways of Bible reading.

The first of these ways is to cover large tracts of Scripture at a single reading; to read carefully, indeed, and with a keen attention; but continuously, without pausing to settle the many perplexing questions which will spring to the mind. It is a useful habit, from time to time as occasion offers, to read through a whole book at a sitting. The value of such continuous and rapid reading is fourfold. It impresses us with the unique dignity and spirituality of the Scriptures, as little else can; it gives a certain familiarity with the contents and language and style of the various books; it fixes in the memory those passages which seem to leap from their contexts, as being of the

(i.) Long passages continuously.

greatest importance or beauty; and it enables us to grasp the main drift of a writer's teaching, and the scope of his argument, and so to attain a right sense of proportion in religious matters.

The second of the ways of reading the Bible is to **(ii.) One book minutely.** study with great care and patience some one selected book; perusing it with a minute attention to details, and making use of all the assistance which happens to be available. It is important to read, first, some introduction, usually to be found in a commentary, which discusses the setting of the book, its authorship, date, the circumstances in which it was written, and the readers for whom it was intended. With that assistance, the student should then plunge into the book, wrestling honestly with its difficulties, analysing its argument, making careful note of the very words and phrases used, and collecting from it the teaching given upon various points of interest. In the course of this study, he should only call in the assistance of commentaries when the problem to be faced completely baffles him, or when he wishes to check or correct his own solutions. But, when once he has finished this arduous first-hand study, then he is at liberty to make use of the labours of others; and he will find that the discipline he has gone through will enable him to profit far more by such labours, than he would ever have done otherwise.

The third way of reading the Bible is also of the **(iii.) One subject pursued through entire Bible.** greatest value. It is to select some one topic or idea, and to pursue it in its growth throughout the entire volume. For this purpose it is necessary to treat the various documents historically, taking them in chronological order, grouping them in accordance with their authorship, and distributing them in view of the localities in which they were written. A study of this kind puts it in the way of the student to obtain a wide and comprehensive grasp of the religious principles and doctrines of the Bible. But, for such a study, the use of concordances, books of reference, and the pursuit of those by-paths of historical research which frequently throw so much light upon the subject in hand, are indispensable.

There is yet a fourth way of reading the Bible, of (iv.) Devotional reading. which we will speak only briefly here; for though it is, in some respects, the most important of all, yet it is not so much a matter of study as of devotion. The method is that of selecting a particular incident, or passage of teaching, and making it the subject of prayerful meditation. Naturally what our previous study has made us to know of the passage will now aid our spiritual insight. But the object in view is, not so much to achieve a critically sound interpretation, as to discover what God would say to ourselves by its means. Without reading our own ideas into the passage, or attempting to force from it an application to our own life; if we store it in our hearts, let our minds dwell constantly upon it, and ponder it deeply, we will often find that presently a light will shine through the darkness, and God's voice will make itself heard. If that were not so, then the Bible could never enter into our life as the dominant factor of our religious experience. Practically, therefore, this is probably the highest method of study. But, since it is eminently uncritical, it must be remembered that the results are personal only, and, though self-evident perhaps to ourselves, of no necessary force to others.

13. But we must return to the all-important position that, because the Bible is a religious book, all study of it should be conducted in a religious spirit. In all branches of learned investigation a great reverence for the particular subject is of fundamental moment. It is only that true sympathy which is based upon reverence that can give the necessary intellectual insight; and the sense of profound awe, which is the mark of every serious student, contributes, more than anything else, to train him in the diligence and intellectual honesty, carefulness and disciplined attention, which are so important for all good work. And if this is true of other departments of study, it is yet more true of the study of the Bible. It is the spiritual understanding which is the true sympathetic attitude in our approach to the reading of Scripture; for that alone can unlock its secrets for us. The scholar, busied upon some perplexing problem of antiquarian lore which has met him in the sacred pages, and careful to sift and weigh his evidence in the dry clear light of reason, is nevertheless aided, and not hindered, in his task by that same devotional attitude. And so our aim, as humble students of Holy Writ, should be to stand always within, and not outside of, the pale of that religious experience which the Bible fosters, and to which it appeals; for only so does the sacred Book become really fruitful to ourselves, and, by our means, to others whom we may be called upon to influence and guide.

But all study should really be devotional.

BIBLIOGRAPHY.

EWALD: 'Revelation: its Nature and Record.' (Trans. Goadby. T. and T. Clark. 1884.)

SANDAY: 'The Oracles of God.' (Longmans, Green. 1891.)

DRIVER: 'Sermons on the Old Testament'; esp. No. 7. (Methuen. 1892.)

GORE: 'The Holy Spirit and Inspiration'; No. 8 in 'Lux Mundi,' ed. Gore. (Murray. 14th ed. 1895.)

KIRKPATRICK: 'The Divine Library of the Old Testament.' (Macmillan. 1896.)

SANDAY: 'Inspiration.' Bampton Lectures, 1893. (Longmans, Green. 3rd ed. 1896.)

FAIRBAIRN: 'The Philosophy of the Christian Religion.' (Hodder and Stoughton. 3rd ed. 1903.)

GARVIE: 'Revelation'; in Hastings' 'Dictionary of the Bible,' extra volume. (T. and T. Clark. 1904.)

WILSON: 'The Idea of Revelation'; No. 6 in 'Cambridge Theological Essays,' ed. Swete. (Macmillan. 1905.)

JOYCE: 'The Inspiration of Prophecy.' (Frowde. 1910.)

WEBB: 'Problems in the Relations of God and Man.' (Nisbet. 1911.)

CHAPTER II

THE TEXT, LITERATURE AND CANON OF THE OLD TESTAMENT

1. IN this chapter we shall attempt to deal with
Three lines of
study.
three more or less distinct branches of Old
Testament criticism; the history of the
text, the history of the literary composition of the
various books, and the history of the Canon. These
three lines of study we shall, so far as is possible,
disentangle the one from the other; but as each one
to some extent implies the others, we shall not be
able to avoid some overlapping in our treatment of
them.

Obviously we must start by defining our terms.
(i.) Textual
Criticism.
By 'Textual Criticism' we mean a study
of the written sources from which we derive
the Hebrew original of our Old Testament translation.
The object of this study is to reach the highest possible
standard of correctness, mainly by ruling out the mistakes
which have crept into the text during a history of many
hundreds of years. This line of study is sometimes
known as the 'lower criticism.' It is a criticism which
is by no means confined to the Bible, but is applied by
scholars to the whole range of literature. Its province is
doubtless more extended in dealing with books of great
antiquity; but there is found to be room and need for it

even in the works of modern authors. Thus, to illustrate the point, in Shelley's *Alastor* the old printed editions have, in line 327, 'wave running on wave'; but what Shelley actually wrote appears to have been, 'wave ruining (i.e. falling into ruins) on wave.' Or again; in *The Revolt of Islam*, Dedication vi, the last line was printed, 'Aught but a lifeless *clog*, until revived by thee,' where the word italicised should have been 'clod.'

If this is 'lower criticism,' then the 'higher criticism' (ii.) Literary Criticism. is a study of the books themselves from a literary point of view; and the object of this study is to discover where, by whom, and when they were written; and to trace back their information, and even their language, to earlier written sources which have now disappeared. This line of study will be familiar to all who have given any attention to the masterpieces of English literature; but we may perhaps briefly illustrate it by giving a few samples of the method as applied to the Shakespearean drama. Thus the fancy, or story, which is the ground-work of *A Midsummer Night's Dream*, was probably appropriated by the author from Chaucer; and it may be traced back to the Roman poet Ovid. Similarly the narrative of *Hamlet* was derived, possibly, from various sources; but, more than this, it appears that the poet depended in large measure, for the construction of his play, upon a previous work by Kyd, some of whose lines he incorporated unaltered (e.g. act III, scene iv, lines 136—141). Or, again, historical research amongst old records appears to have demonstrated that *King Lear* was first acted on 26th December 1606; and that it was, in all probability, written for that occasion.

The Greek word 'canon,' derived from 'canna,' a reed, originally meant a straight rule or measure; and in course of time, owing to the very different things which could be measured and the divers senses in which measurement was possible, it came to mean a test or a standard. When applied to the Scriptures the word has two senses; either that the Sacred Writings are to be accepted as the rule and standard of a devout and God-fearing life; or that they alone are to be judged the books which fully satisfy the test of inspiration. It is with this last sense that we are principally concerned here. And by the criticism, or history, of the Canon, we mean a study of the process by which certain books were selected and set apart as being, in a peculiar degree, inspired by God. It is not possible, from the nature of the case, to illustrate this by the production of examples which are precisely similar. The nearest approach, by way of analogy, is perhaps that which we call literary taste or appreciation. Why, we may ask, does the ordinary reader confine himself to, let us say, *Robinson Crusoe* and *Gulliver's Travels*, and neglect the other writings of Defoe and Swift? To some extent, we may answer, because he applies, almost unconsciously, a certain test to all literary productions. In other words, there is a canon of literary value, not wholly unlike that which has attributed inspiration to the Biblical writings.

(iii.) Criticism of the Canon.

2. Having thus defined our terms, we must now go on to exhibit the application of these three kinds of criticism to the Scriptures themselves. But to understand aright the problems of textual criticism, it is necessary that we should first say a few words about the Hebrew language. The people who

The Hebrew Language.

are known to history as the 'Hebrews' before the
Babylonian captivity, and as the 'Jews' after their
return from exile, were a branch of the great Semitic
race. To this race belonged some of the greatest nations
of antiquity; the Babylonians, from whom the Assyrians
were probably an off-shoot, the Egyptians, the Canaanites,
Aramaeans, and others. All the evidence available seems
to point to the fact that the Semites originated in the
interior of Arabia; and from thence they gradually
spread, by successive waves of immigration, all over
the near east. What their original language was it is
impossible for us to say; for, in the earliest times to
which the records take us, it was already diversified in
a number of distinct tongues. The speeches current in
Palestine before the advent of the Hebrews were the
Phoenician and the Canaanite; and to these, as we
gather from the few inscriptions which have been preserved, the Hebrew was near akin. The peoples to
the north possessed a language known as Aramaic; a
language in which a few brief passages of the Old
Testament are written (i.e. Ezra iv. 8—vi. 18; vii. 12—26:
Daniel ii. 4—vii. 28). This is the language referred to
under the name 'Chaldee,' but wrongly so; for the
Chaldeans were a non-Semitic race who occupied territories in Southern Babylonia, round the head of the
Persian Gulf. A later form of the Aramaic was Syriac,
in which many early Christian books were written. The
Samaritan language was also a dialect of the Aramaic.
Gradually in Palestine the Hebrew gave place to Aramaic,
until the time came that the Jews no longer spoke their
native tongue. It was a dead language, just as Latin is
to us; though, again like Latin, it was for a long time
used for literary purposes, and afterwards still continued

to be studied in the schools. Precisely why, or when, this change took place we cannot say; but there is no doubt that Hebrew was no longer understood, and Aramaic alone spoken, by the people in the days of our Lord; and a very great deal of early Jewish litera- ture, written after the destruction of the Temple, is in Aramaic.

3. The Assyrians and Babylonians possessed their 'cuneiform' (wedge-shaped) writing, and the Egyptians their 'hieroglyphic' (sacred carving); but these were either pictures, or symbols of ideas, or characters denoting syllables. When and where alphabetic writing originated is quite unknown. But the earliest people to possess such a writing, so far as we know at present, were the Phoenicians; and they had it in common use by the year 1500 B.C. The Phoenician alphabet is the parent of the Hebrew as well as of the Greek. In fact the earliest Hebrew inscription which has come to light, the Gezer tablet which perhaps belongs to the 8th century B.C., differs very little from the Phoenician.

The Hebrew Script.

We have no means of judging when the Hebrews first practised the art of writing. It is of course possible that their officials may have used the Babylonian cuneiform before they came to adopt the Phoenician alphabet; but of this we have no evidence. And it is quite unlikely that any part of the Old Testament ever saw the light in the cuneiform script. We must recollect that the early Hebrews were not possessed of any high degree of culture and civili- sation; and that they would not have been likely to acquire the art of writing until they had been leading a settled life for some considerable period of time. But

(a) Antiquity.

that art, as the possession of the few, was probably laying the foundations of a future Hebrew literature by the period of the beginning of the monarchy, i.e. circ. 1000 B.C.

The earliest form of the Hebrew script was, as we have noticed, very similar to the Phoenician; and it bears little resemblance to the square characters with which we are familiar at the present day. The square characters are, in their origin, Aramaean; and the probability is that, when the Hebrew language began to be supplanted by the Aramaic, the Aramaean script would, first of all, have been used for the ordinary purposes of daily life, and then very gradually have ousted the Hebrew script in the writing of the Scriptures. Both forms of writing, as both languages, would have been in use side by side for a considerable period; and we can only give the outside dates of this process. The Samaritan Bible is, to the present day, written in the old Hebrew script; which is evidence that that script was alone used at the time when the Samaritans came by their Bible; i.e. not earlier than circ. 400 B.C. On the other hand it seems probable that the square characters were alone in use, at least for the writing of the Scriptures, in the times of our Lord.

(b) Forms.

Like other Semitic languages, the Hebrew alphabet differs from our own in that it possesses no characters for the vowel sounds; it is entirely an alphabet of consonants. While Hebrew, the native language of the people who produced this literature, was still generally spoken, this would have presented no difficulties. But when Hebrew became a dead language; and when, at a later date, it was only

(c) Vowel pointing.

acquired by scholars whose native tongue was, perhaps, Greek; then it became a serious problem how the Hebrew of the Old Testament was to be pronounced. And this was more than a question of casual interest; for, in several cases where the consonantal spelling of words was identical or very similar, the supplying of the vowels seriously affected the sense of the passages in which those words occurred. To meet this difficulty Jewish scholars, somewhere between the years 600 and 700 A.D., invented an elaborate system of points and lines, to represent vowel sounds and accents; the object of which was to assist the reader to a right pronunciation, and therefore a right understanding, of the Holy Scriptures in which they were inserted. These vowel points were suggested by, if not borrowed from, the Syriac; and the pronunciation they indicated was that which had been handed down orally from scholar to scholar; and the system was thus known as ' Massorah ' (= tradition).

4. By the opening of the Christian era, and probably

Standard Text. a hundred years previously, the collection of the Scriptures had become invested with a very high degree of sanctity. The great, and increasing, reverence which was felt for them led up to the theory that every phrase, word or letter, had its peculiar value, and must therefore be guarded with extraordinary diligence. It was one of the functions of the Scribes to see to it that an exact and accurate text was transmitted from generation to generation, free from all the natural errors of the copyists and the additions which some might be tempted to make. They consulted and compared all the existing manuscripts they could lay their hands upon; and, wherever they found different readings, they decided in favour of the one which was supported by the greatest number of manuscripts. Thus they built up a certain type of text, which became the parent of the one we now possess; and they probably destroyed all previously-existing copies of the various books.

5. It is not to be supposed that the work of the Scribes was free from all errors. The Samaritan Bible consists of the Pentateuch (i.e. Genesis to Deuteronomy) only; and a comparison of the above type of text with this exhibits many differences; though, owing to the fact that the Pentateuch was held to be sacred before any of the other books, and was always preserved with greater care, these differences are not very considerable. But we possess a Greek translation of the Hebrew Bible, known as the Septuagint (so called because legend had it that the translation was the work of seventy scholars, and generally referred to by the symbol LXX), which was made in successive stages between the years 250 and 132 B.C. This translation differs, in some places, very widely from the text we possess; and was evidently made from manuscripts which were discarded. In addition to this, it appears that many readings which the Scribes set aside were handed down by tradition, and were often read instead of what stood in the text. The Massoretes (i.e. the guardians of the Massorah of the 6th century) inserted these other readings, together with corrections of their own, in the margins of their manuscripts, though they did not venture to alter the consonantal text itself. These marginal readings were known as Qrîs (= that which is read); the corresponding words in the text being the Kthîbh (= that which is written). It will be

Room for correction.

seen, from what we have said, that the actual Hebrew text which we possess is not altogether to be depended upon ; and that it is possible, in some cases, to find, from these different sources, readings which are more satisfactory, and which probably represent more exactly what the original authors wrote.

6. In the Old Testament we find frequent references **Manuscripts.** to 'rolls' where we should speak of 'books.' The explanation of this is found in the ancient custom of writing upon strips of skin or leather, which were attached to two wooden rollers, one at either end, for the convenience of the reader. Each book of the Old Testament was, at one time, written upon a separate roll ; though, before the next transition took place, some of the shorter books were undoubtedly combined. It is of interest to notice that the five books, 'Song of Songs,' 'Ruth,' 'Lamentations,' 'Ecclesiastes,' and 'Esther,' still bear their old title of the 'Five Megilloth' (= Rolls) ; and also, that in modern Jewish synagogues the Torah (= Law, i.e. the Pentateuch) is still read from rolls.

It is probable that the Scriptures began to be written on papyrus and parchment in the first Christian century ; and, as time went on, the various parchments were bound together in the form of a book, so that the Old Testament now appeared for the first time as a single volume. The invention of the art of printing took place in the year 1454 ; and the first portion of the Bible to be printed in Hebrew was an edition of the Psalms, which was produced at Bologna in 1477. From that time forward the whole of the Hebrew Bible has been printed over and over again. These printed editions are all founded upon the manuscript books which preceded them ; and they, in turn, are all exact transcriptions of the Massoretic text, which goes back, so far as the consonants are concerned, without change to about 100 B.C.

7. But the manuscripts which have come down to
Their antiquity. us are none of them of very ancient date. It is generally supposed that the oldest of all, a manuscript of the Prophets now at St Petersburg, may be dated 916 A.D. The comparatively recent date of the Old Testament manuscripts, as compared with those of the New Testament, demands some explanation; and that explanation is not far to seek. In the first place, the great care which was always taken to maintain a very high standard of transcription, and the ruthless destruction of faulty copies, probably resulted in a small production. Of these, a very large number would have perished in the natural course of events, through usage and the lapse of time. It is true that there was usually to be found in the synagogues a cellar, called 'geniza' or hiding-place, where were stored the worn copies of the Scriptures, which reverence forbade the Jews to destroy, and the fear of imperfection did not allow them to retain in circulation; but this did not as a rule conspire to their preservation, but rather the reverse. And, beside this, we know that the fanatical persecution of the Jews by Christians in the middle ages, especially during the period of the crusades, led to the wanton and wholesale destruction of the sacred books.

8. We have already referred in passing to the
The Versions. Samaritan Pentateuch and the Greek Septuagint; and we must now devote a little space to dealing more particularly with the various ancient translations, or versions, of the Old Testament.

Of the Samaritan it is unnecessary to say more here,
(i.) The   than to emphasise the fact that in the
Samaritan.   places where it is found to differ from the
Massoretic text its evidence is of great importance,
owing to the early date at which it was produced.
But to the LXX and the rest we must devote more time.

There are in existence a number of Aramaic transla-
                         tions of the Scriptures, known by the name
(ii.) The
Aramaic   of Targums.   In some cases these are
Targums.
                         literal renderings of the Hebrew ; in others
they are mere paraphrases ; and they contain a good
deal of matter not found in the Scriptures at all.   The
dates of their composition and the names of their authors
are alike unknown ; for the names they bear are quite
untrustworthy.   They appear to have originated in
Palestine, and they are written in the Aramaic dialect
which was spoken in that locality; but it seems that they
were not admitted to the Palestinian synagogues until
they had long been in use in the eastern, or Babylonian,
dispersion.   When Hebrew had ceased to be a spoken
language, it became necessary to translate the portions
of Scripture read at the synagogue services into Aramaic,
for the edification of the congregation ; but for a long
while these translations were not committed to writing,
but were orally preserved.   Nevertheless, though the
Targums are probably none of them earlier than the
5th century A.D., it is probable that they contain much
valuable material ; renderings, that is to say, of Hebrew
MSS which have perished ; and thus they may be used,
with caution, for textual purposes.   The four principal
Targums are those of Onkelos and Jonathan, the 1st
Jerusalem (also known as Pseudo-Jonathan), and the
2nd Jerusalem.   The two Jerusalem Targums, which

seem to be considerably later than the others, together with Onkelos, contain the Pentateuch ; while Jonathan is a translation of the Prophets.

But the place of primary importance must be given (iii.) The Greek to the Greek versions, and particularly to Versions; that one which is known as the Septuagint. especially the LXX. The story of this translation is related in a Greek work, the so-called ' Letter of Aristeas,' which ascribes the labour to seventy select scholars who undertook it at the instance of the Egyptian King Ptolemy Philadelphus, circ. 250 B.C. But the ' Letter of Aristeas ' is certainly a Jewish forgery, and the information it conveys is, in the main, pure fiction. It is not difficult to see what were the reasons which led to a Greek translation of the Scriptures being made. The fact that an ever-increasing number of Jews were living away from their own country, in lands where Aramaic was unfamiliar and Greek was the language of daily life, meant that, in course of time, to a large section of the peculiar people Aramaic and the sacred Hebrew were quite unknown, and the Scriptures were rapidly becoming a sealed book. This, and perhaps the desire that the inspired writings should become known to the cultured understanding of the West, was a sufficient cause for the work of translation being undertaken ; a work which may indeed have commenced under the auspices of an enlightened monarch about 250 B.C., but which was not accomplished all at once, being, rather, spread over nearly a hundred and fifty years, and distributed amongst a number of unknown scholars during that period.

The LXX was thus antecedent to the Massoretic type of text, and is an invaluable witness to the readings of many Hebrew MSS which the Massoretes discarded. But its value must not be over-estimated ; for the translation is clearly of very unequal care and merit, and in many places obviously sits very loosely to the original. It was owing partly to this freedom of rendering, and still more to the Christian use of the LXX, that a general distrust of it was awakened in the Jewish mind, so that in the 2nd century A.D. there was a loud call for a revised translation which should be more literal and exact. Many attempts were made to meet this demand ; and fragments of three of these have survived to our own days ; the versions namely of Aquila, of Theodotion and of Symmachus. These are all, and especially the first, characterised by extreme literality ; and, since they too are independent of the Massoretic text, their value for critical purposes is high.

The Greek versions were never accorded the reverence, and therefore the care in preservation, which belonged as of right to the Hebrew original. And the consequence of this has been that the text has become very much corrupted: and the different MSS record a great variety of readings. Now it is obvious that, if we are to use the Greek versions for restoring the original Hebrew, it is necessary first to settle beyond dispute the correct texts of those versions. The labour entailed in this task is very similar to that involved in restoring the original text of the New Testament; four of the principal MSS also of the New Testament are our primary authorities for the Old (i.e. those known as א, A, B and C); and it will probably suffice to refer the reader to the next chapter for an explanation of this critical task. But here we may add that, as regards the LXX, there appear to have been three separate editions of the text in ancient

days, which are in different degrees represented by all
the extant MSS. There was that of Origen, to be dated
about 250 A.D., which had as its province Caesarea and
Palestine; there was the edition of Lucian (circ. 300 A.D.),
belonging to Antioch and Syria; and there was that of
Hesychius (circ. 300 A.D.), which emanated from Alexandria and Egypt. Owing in part to the lack of sanctity
attaching to the LXX version, and the absence of that
jealous guardianship which watched the fortunes of the
Hebrew Scriptures, there came to be attached to it a
number of other writings, mainly, if not wholly, of Greek
composition, which never found a place in the Hebrew
Canon of the Old Testament. Of these we shall have
something to say at a later stage; but here it will be
sufficient to observe that they have for the most part
found their way into our Apocrypha, and that it was the
almost exclusive use of the Greek Bible by the early
Christian Church which happily preserved them for us as
being of quasi-canonical authority.

The other versions of the Old Testament concern
us very little, for they have only a slight
use for the textual critic. The chief of
these versions are, the Syriac, which exists
(iv.) The Syriac, Coptic and Latin Versions.
in two forms, the Peshitto and the Syro-Hexaplar; the
Coptic, which exists in the two main dialects of Egypt;
and the Latin, of which there are the two forms, known
as the Old Latin and Jerome's Vulgate. These versions
were probably all of them the work of Christian mis-
sionaries and scholars; and they were for the most part
translated, not directly from the Hebrew, but from the
existing Greek versions. It is true that Jerome translated afresh out of the Hebrew; but the basis of his work
was the Massoretic text.

9. We are now in a position to understand, some-
The function
of Textual
Criticism. what, the province and scope of the textual
criticism of the Old Testament. It is, first
of all, by a very thorough examination of
all the existing MSS and printed editions, to establish
what was precisely the Massoretic text of, say, the
seventh century A.D., with all its vowel points and
accents. This has, for all practical purposes, already
been achieved; and since it is obviously necessary for
the student to work upon the most correct text he can
obtain, we may regard this as one of the most valuable
of the fruits of modern scholarship. But, to go behind
this text which is only a type, neither early nor critical,
the scholar must take into account the marginal Qrîs of
the Massorah, the evidence of all the versions, and the
quotations from, and comments upon, the Scriptures in
the early Jewish writings, Mishnah, Gemara and Midrashim, of which we shall give some account in another
place. By these means he will be able to correct many
obvious mistakes, and clear up a host of difficulties and
obscurities. But, in addition to this, there will still lie
before him a large field for the use of conjecture in the
production of emendations to a corrupt or mutilated text.
Such emendations may be of different kinds, suggested
by very different lines of study. For instance, a very
careful study of the natural errors to which scribes were
prone in their copying of the Hebrew characters, will
lead the scholar to classify them and reduce them to a
sort of system; from which he may argue that, in some
given place, a suggested reading is more probable than
any that has come down to us, and support his contention by explaining how the faulty reading crept into
the text. Or again; Hebrew poetry was composed in

accordance with definite laws, of measure and parallel clauses; and, where the existing form of a poem is obviously faulty, a just appreciation of the rules governing its construction may assist the scholar to emend its faults. Or once more, from quite a different point of view to the literary; when we remember that the Hebrew tribes were originally nomadic, that they came to settle in territory foreign to them, that they inhabited that land for some hundreds of years, in the course of which its face was completely altered on several occasions by wars and conquests and changes in the character of the population, and that they themselves, during this long period, went through a very remarkable development; and when we recollect that a great part of what was written was first handed down orally for hundreds of years, and that the writings were afterwards frequently revised; and if we further bear in mind the natural tendency to suit old tales to modern conditions, and to supply familiar settings and designations for those which had become strange, and of which the meaning had been forgotten: in view of such facts as these, we shall see that there is scope for the scholar, equipped by a wide knowledge of mythology, archaeology, comparative religion and so forth, who would attempt to restore for us the original names of places, tribes, deities and persons, where these have been obscured; and so to bring once more into the realm of history tribal and religious connections and meanings which have for ages been lost. Such then is, in brief, the function of textual criticism.

10. We may now pass on to consider, more fully, what is meant by the literary, or 'higher,' criticism of the Old Testament. The study

Literary Criticism.

of the literature of any country or people, especially in cases where the production of that literature has been spread over many hundreds of years, makes us familiar with all the following features. The language itself, we find, has undergone a certain development; so that many words and constructions of the earlier period have, in modern times, become obsolete or archaic. Thus, the language of Chaucer is not that of Tennyson. The latter, for instance, would not have used the word 'parementz' (= ornaments); nor would he have written such lines as:—

> 'I saugh today a corps yborn to chirche
> That now on Monday last I saugh him wirche.'

Again: ideas, on religious and social matters, change with the movement of time; so that the views we find expressed in later writers are quite foreign and unknown to the earlier; while many of the allusions in old writers are matters of antiquarian study to present-day students. Thus, our modern views on such a subject as that of representative government would be absolutely unintelligible to an author of the feudal period; and it needs some research to discover what was intended by an ancient writer when he spoke of, let us say, a 'frith stool.' And, once more, not only do different subjects involve different styles of writing in the treatment of them; but individual writers of each generation have their peculiarities, and a style which is more or less their own. Thus, productions so different in character as a legal document, a diary, a newspaper article, or a theological treatise, employ each of them a distinctive diction; and, to mention only two contemporary English writers, it would be impossible to confound the work of Ruskin with that of Carlyle. Now all these features, which appear in the literatures of other races, we shall naturally expect to find reproduced in the Hebrew writings; and our expectation is not disappointed.

11. But, in the Hebrew books, not only do we find all these differences, in language, ideas and style, when we compare one book with another; we also find them in one and the same book, when we compare one portion of it with another. And it is for this reason that we conclude that many of these books are not originally complete works, written by a single author at one definite time; but that they are rather compilations from various sources, achieved by several editors, who have added to, and rearranged, their material through the course of a great many years. And this conclusion is made more certain when we notice various contradictions in, perhaps, two separate accounts of the same event; and when we observe, also, that the different writers treat their subjects from different points of view.

Compilation.

12. If this is so, it is very important that we should be able to dissect these books, apportioning them to the various sources from which they are constructed; and to learn when and where those sources were originally written, and, if possible, by whom; for, by doing so, we shall then be in a better position to understand and interpret our authors. This is a task of very considerable difficulty; and it is only possible here to give the barest outline of the sort of conclusions which scholars have reached.

Analysis.

13. If we begin with the Pentateuch (to which we must add the historical books, except Chronicles, Ezra and Nehemiah), we find that four main documents were used in its composition.

Documents.

The first of these is known as the 'Jehovistic,' and the second as the 'Elohistic'; or, in short, J and E. A word should be given to the explanation of these titles. In primitive times the Hebrews had a name for their God, which was written with the four letters YHVH ; just as the Greeks, for instance, knew their gods by personal names ; e.g. Zeus, Apollo, Pluto and the rest. But in later days, from a feeling of reverence or superstition which is common to uncivilised races, they abstained from mentioning this name. Consequently the pronunciation and meaning of it were soon lost ; and the author of E, in Ex. iii. 14, guesses that it meant " I will be," and was pronounced 'Yāhveh' ('Jehovah' is incorrect). Thus, when it was necessary to speak or write of Him, the word 'Elohim' was often used ; and, at a later time, the vowel points of 'Adonay' were put under YHVH wherever it occurred, to show that this word was to be read in its place. 'Elohim' and 'Adonay' mean, respectively, 'God' and 'Lord.' Now the document we call J employs the sacred name YHVH for God ; while E consistently eschews it, and uses Elohim in its place. Thus there is the probability that J was an earlier document than E.

The other two main sources, to which we have referred, are, first, the Priestly Code, usually known as P ; and, second, the Deuteronomist, for which the symbol D is employed. The latter document is called Deuteronomist for the simple reason that almost the whole of what we possess of it is comprised in our book Deuteronomy ; while the former is known as the Priestly Code because of the nature of its contents, which are in the main concerned with matters of the priesthood, sacrifice, the ritual of worship, and so forth.

If P may be ascribed to priestly authorship, the other three documents are the work of prophets, or their disciples. Their point of view is found to be rather different.

Now the document called J was, in itself, not *(a)* Jehovist the work of a single author; but was document. probably slowly compiled, by constant additions, in the two hundred and fifty years between 900 and 650 B.C. It seems to have emanated from the southern kingdom of Judah. It reflects a very primitive state of society, and, as we should say, somewhat elementary theological ideas. It probably included certain laws and songs (e.g. Ex. xxxiv. 10—27; Gen. xlix) from previous written sources. We do not possess this document in its entirety; but we find it running through Genesis, Exodus, Numbers, Joshua and Judges; it includes Deut. xxxiv, and perhaps may be traced in Samuel.

The document known as E has a shorter history. *(b)* Elohist It is later than J, but must have been document. brought to a completion some while before the fall of Samaria in 721 B.C., for it comes to us from Ephraim, the northern kingdom. Its composition, then, probably fell between the years 850 and 750 B.C. It exhibits an improvement in the social conditions of the people, and reaches a higher range of theological ideas than J. It included ancient written laws and poems; e.g. the section Ex. xx. 20—xxiii. 33, which is known as 'The Book of the Covenant,' and the 'Song of Moses' in Ex. xv. 1—18. Copious extracts from it are to be found in Genesis, Exodus, Numbers, Deuteronomy, Joshua, Judges, and Samuel; and it is probable that the narratives of Elijah and Elisha in Kings were derived from E.

The kernel of the book Deuteronomy is chapters
(c) Deutero- v—xxviii, to which additions were subse-
nomist. quently made. It is quite probable, though
not demonstrable, that this was the law-book discovered
in the Temple in the reign of Josiah, i.e. 621 B.C. If so,
then that portion of the document D was written in
Judah some while previous to that date; possibly in
the reign of Hezekiah, circ. 680 B.C. The document
was considerably added to and expanded during the
Babylonian exile, but attained its final form before the
first captives returned to their native land, in 536 B.C.;
or at any rate before the coming of Nehemiah in 445 B.C.
To it belong the greater part of our book Deuteronomy,
some small portions of Genesis, Exodus, Numbers and
Samuel; and large sections of Joshua, Judges and
Kings. The writers attain a high level of spirituality;
and, in presenting a code of law, use all the arts of
moral suasion to inculcate obedience to it.

The Priestly Code embraces a great deal of the
(d) Priestly material found in Genesis, Exodus and
Code. Numbers, the whole of Leviticus, and
Joshua xiii—xxii. Its main characteristic is its legal
language, with the regular recurrence of technical terms
and formulas. It traces back the whole system of law
to the authority of Moses, both on its religious and its
civil side. It has much in common with the book of
Ezekiel. There can be little doubt that it was composed
in Babylonia, subsequent to Deuteronomy and after the
exile, but before the mission of Ezra to Jerusalem in or
about 400 B.C. It contains an older document, generally
known as 'The Law of Holiness' (H for short), which
is to be found in Lev. xvii—xxvi; a code of laws
dependent to some extent upon 'The Book of the

Covenant,' but more closely connected with Ez. xl—xlviii.
'Holiness' or 'sanctity' is the main idea underlying
these laws; hence the name. It was probably compiled
in Babylonia during the exile, from older sources.

Other sources than these four seem to have been
(e) Combina-   used in the compilation of our present books;
tion of these.   and the hands of editors, or redactors, may
be detected dove-tailing one document into another.
It would, however, carry us too far afield to follow out
the intricate processes of combination here; and it must
suffice to say that the evidence goes to show that the
various sources were only brought together very gradually.
First J and E were combined, some time between 650 B.C.
and the beginning of the Babylonian exile. Then, during
the exile, JE was linked on to D. And, last of all, P
was added to JED at some time subsequent to the
exile, possibly before 398 B.C., when it seems that Ezra
proclaimed the Law to the people, but more probably
a few years later.

The same process of analysis applied to the pro-
(f) Prophetic   phetical books produces, in certain cases,
writings;   similar results. The book of Isaiah, for
e.g. Isaiah.   instance, is a case in point; and it may
be well to give here a rough account of the distribution
of the different prophecies it contains, though it should
be clearly understood that the account is not equally
trustworthy in all its parts. The sections which may
confidently be ascribed to Isaiah himself are i—xi. 9;
xiv. 24—xx. 6 (of which xv and xvi are adaptations of
an older prophecy); xxi. 11—xxiii. 18; and xxviii—
xxxii. To these have been added certain prophecies
not by Isaiah; xi. 10—xiv. 23, which belongs to the
period of the exile; xxiv—xxvii, which may be

attributed to the times of Ezra; and xxi. 1—10, xxxiii—xxxv, which are also post-exilic. These collected prophecies of Isaiah, mingled with the later non-Isaianic additions, appear to have formed three independent groups, i—xii, xiii—xxiii, and xxiv—xxxv, which at some date subsequent to the exile were combined in a single book, to which the editor appended the historical narrative, found in xxxvi—xxxix, culled from the book of Kings. The whole then went by the name of Isaiah. The remaining chapters form two distinct groups, which are now ordinarily termed Deutero-Isaiah (xl—lv) and Trito-Isaiah (lvi—lxvi). The first of these contains the sections which are designated the Servant Passages; namely xlii. 1—7; xlix. 1—13; l. 4—11; and lii. 13—liii. 12. It is probable that these passages are extracts from an independent poem, which may be as late as the Maccabaean period. The Deutero-Isaiah group falls into two divisions; xl—xlviii, which is late exilic, and xlix—lv, which is immediately post-exilic; and it seems probable that the Servant Passages were inserted by the editor who combined these two divisions. The Trito-Isaiah group, lvi—lxvi, consists of a number of separate prophecies belonging to various historical occasions; but all of them are post-exilic. It seems that the Deutero- and Trito-Isaiah were first combined; and, then, that it was simply the accident of juxtaposition which led to the combination of the anonymous xl—lxvi with the Isaianic book i—xxxix.

If we turn to other of the Old Testament books, again we meet with evidence of the same *(g)* Other books; sort of editorial work. Our present book e.g. Psalms. of Psalms, for instance, is a collection made, probably, in the Maccabaean period. This collection was founded upon several earlier and smaller psalters, the contents of which it appropriated and rearranged; and it doubtless included a number of Psalms which had hitherto remained independent. There are certain indications, in the titles of the Psalms, which enable us to apportion them to their original collections; and we gather that the object of such collections was the provision of hymns for use in the Temple worship. Doubtless some few of our Psalms may legitimately be ascribed to the authorship of David; but the greater part of them, ranging as they do over a long period of time, are of post-exilic date; and some may have been composed so late as the days of the Maccabees. Further; an examination of the text and structure of the Psalms reveals that, in several cases, we have not the poems as they originally stood, but the combination of earlier psalms by the hand of a later editor.

14. But it is unnecessary, here, to explore further the intricacies of this literary analysis. It is sufficient for our purpose to have noted this very characteristic feature in Hebrew writings; the constant use of scissors and paste, as it were, in the piecing together of already existing documents, and the habit of making additions to, or otherwise colouring, the sources as it seemed good to the various editors. And we should remark that this ancient people had not arrived at the comparatively modern idea, which regards an author's work as his property, and forbids the loan and use of the fruits of his labour without leave being obtained, or a fitting acknowledgement made. In those days, it is evident that literature in every form was regarded as a national possession, the property of all alike.

Plagiarism.

15. And, in passing, we should draw attention to
The question of Authorship. another fact of some importance, which is in a manner related to this. The Jews were accustomed to speak of their Law as being by Moses, their Psalmody by David, their Proverbial Wisdom by Solomon; and there was a tendency to group their Prophecy under the name of Isaiah, and, in the extra-canonical literature, the Apocalyptic writings under that of Enoch. Undoubtedly in the first century of our era it was customary to understand this in a strictly literal sense; and a Mosaic or Davidic author-ship was imputed to all that happened to have been gathered under those great names. But modern literary criticism has clearly demonstrated the impossibility of this, and we are driven to discover a reason for such a curious literary custom. Nor is this reason hard to find. Tradition had always associated the name of Moses with the giving of the Law; and, when the existing laws of the Hebrews came to be codified and written down, it would have seemed obvious, to those who had no know-ledge of the past origin and growth of the whole system of law and custom, that what was written was essentially what Moses had delivered. At a later time groups of laws, or different codes, were brought together and inter-mingled; and when this process had passed out of mind, and it became impossible to distinguish one element from another, the whole came to be attributed to Moses, and it was even asserted that it came from his hand. With regard to the Proverbs, Psalms or Prophecies, the case is not very different. A collection was made, let us say, of Psalms, which contained some pieces of indisputable Davidic authorship, besides a number of poems which were by lesser men, or altogether

anonymous. It would have been natural to call this collection by the name of its most important contributor; and that, again, would have led to the popular ascription of the whole to him. But, when once he came to be the reputed author of a collection of writings, it would have easily transpired that, in course of time, a whole anonymous literature would have been put under the shelter of his name, since no other was known who could compete in fame with the royal psalmist. And this, in turn, would have fostered a well-known literary device. In an age when the products of literature were not regarded as a private possession of the author, and when certainly the majority of pieces were issued anonymously, it became customary for the author to put out his work under the name of the most famous of the authors of antiquity, or, in the case of an Enoch for instance, of those who might be presumed to be peculiarly cognisant of the matter of which he was writing. And this he did, not by way of deception, or in order to suggest that such a man was in reality the author of the work; but rather by way of implying that the work represented the teaching, and in a measure the genius, of the reputed author, and in order to gain a hearing for an unnamed Elisha upon whom the mantle of an Elijah was presumed to have fallen. There are literary analogies which to some extent support this view of the case. For instance, there appears to have existed a whole literature which went under the name of the mythical Orpheus; and a number of spurious plays for a long while claimed Shakespeare as their author.

16. It is at this point that we must bring into our
History of the enquiry the history of the growth of the
Canon. Old Testament Canon. This is bound up

with the problems of literary criticism to a very large extent; for the history of the composition of the books is, from one point of view, the history of their acceptance as Scripture. We must, first of all, clear the ground by making two remarks of a general nature, which are however of great importance for the understanding of our subject.

17. The first of these has to do with the period

The Oral Stage. during which a great deal of what we now possess in the Old Testament existed, before it was ever put into writing. In the case of the earliest Hebrew literature, we must remember that it deals with historical times long antecedent to those in which the first literary productions appeared, and during which the Hebrews were entirely ignorant of the art of writing. It is undoubtedly true that the written sources themselves are coloured by the ideas, religious and social, of the age in which they were composed; and it is not always easy to say how far they can be used as evidence for the customs and practices of an earlier age. But it is also true that they embody a great deal of far older material, some of which was already no longer understood when it came to be recorded in writing. Now this older material had clearly passed through a long and eventful history before ever it was dealt with by an author's pen. In other words, a great deal of what we now possess must have been learnt by heart, and handed down from generation to generation; just as the minstrels of the middle ages, or the professional story-tellers in the East at the present day, pass on their stock-in-trade by oral delivery. And this does not apply to the earliest historical period only. It is also true of a great range of prophecy, that it was

treasured by the prophet's disciples, and orally com-
municated to others, before it at length found a literary
form.   And it is obviously the case with proverbial
wisdom, that what we possess is the result of a diligent
collection of sayings that had for ages been on people's
tongues.   To the western mind it is almost incredible
that so much of history, law and so forth, could have
been stored in the memory, and handed on by oral
delivery with such extraordinary accuracy as we know
to have been the case.   But that the feat was not
impossible is witnessed by a similar fact which belongs
to the history of the later Rabbinical literature.   The
Jewish Talmud is a work of enormous bulk, and consists
of two principal elements ; the Mishnah, or 'teaching,'
which embraces a large number of tracts on very various
subjects, and embodies the scribal additions to the
Canonical Law-books which had accumulated through
the centuries ; and the Gemara, or 'supplement,' which
is a collection of the Rabbinical comments upon, and
expansions or interpretations of, the Mishnah.   Now
the whole of this was carried in the memory, as it
appears, and handed down for generations by word of
mouth ; and it was certainly not committed to writing
until after the 6th century A.D.

18.   The other preliminary remark we have to make
is this.   We must not suppose that the
Old Testament represents the whole of
Hebrew and Jewish literature, up to the
time when the Canon was closed.   There
can be no doubt that there existed, at one
time and another, a large range of literature which has
entirely disappeared.   In the first place, the editors of
our various books of composite origin did not use up

The process of
selection, by
religious in-
stinct, and
conscious
appeal to re-
ligious sense.

the sources they brought together ; for, had they done so, it would have been possible for us to reconstruct those documents entirely ; and this we cannot do. Then, we notice frequent references in the historical books to works of which we know nothing ; such as 'The Book of Jasher,' 'The Acts of the Kings of Israel,' 'The Words of Nathan the Prophet,' and 'The Vision of Iddo the Seer'—to mention but a few of them (cp. Eccles. xii. 12). And, in addition to this, we still possess a few books of the later period, which were never regarded as forming any part of the Jewish Scriptures ; 'The Book of Enoch' for instance, 'The Psalms of Solomon,' 'The Book of Jubilees,' and 'The Testaments of the Twelve Patriarchs'; beside certain of the works which have found their way into our Apocrypha.

Now, since it is true that the Old Testament only forms a part of the whole of Hebrew literature ; we desire to know in what manner our books were preserved where so much else has perished, and why they acquired a character of peculiar sanctity. The history of the formation of the Canon is really an answer to this question. But it is important, in this connection, to observe that the books we possess are not the mere relics of a literature,—just, as we might say, what happened to escape the ravages of time. A comparison with the surviving literatures of Babylonia or Greece, which contain works on magic and astrology, mathematics and medicine, forbids us to suppose such a thing; for the Hebrew books have, as a whole, a definite religious character; and mere chance would not have preserved these only, and none of a different stamp. Nor is the Old Testament a collection only of the gems and masterpieces of Hebrew work; for, in the first place, it would not be possible to define codes of law and genealogies by such a term ; and, in the second place, it must surely have been that Hebrew literature possessed other such beautiful pieces as Ruth and the Song of Songs, which nevertheless have not come down to us.

It seems to be clear that in some cases the books, or the sources from which they were compiled, were not written under the consciousness that they were, or would become, sacred literature. In such cases (and we may cite Esther, the Song of Songs, and the sources of Ezra, as examples) they would have been selected, very gradually, from a great mass of writings covering a very large range of subjects, either because of certain inherent qualities they were seen to possess, or because their editor found in them the material he required for his own religious purpose. In other cases, however, it would seem that the books were issued in the first instance as possessing a Divine authority, and were received by the people as such ; or they were composed of documents which already were assumed to possess this character. The Priestly Code was promulgated by Ezra, and was accepted by his hearers, as being the very voice of God; and to some extent, doubtless, the name and authority of Moses, to whom tradition ascribed its matter, would have guaranteed its Divine character. The prophetical writings, again, whether committed to literary form by the prophet himself or set down by his disciples after his death, at any rate made their appearance with the distinct claim to be inspired, and under the auspices of the prophetical schools; and, from the time of the exile onwards, the people were, as a whole, inclined to reverence and give ear to their prophets.

Moreover the prestige of these prophetical schools, from which they emanated, would have given an assured position to the historical books, which were less formal histories than illustrative accounts of the operations of the Divine in human affairs. Thus we may discern several forces at work in the building up of the library of the Old Testament; a force which we may call that of natural selection, which separated out, here and there, a document, holding a place in the national literature, for its peculiar religious depth or significance; the force of the prophetic character and mission; the force attaching to the glamour of a great name; and the force which belongs of right to ecclesiastical authority. But we may safely say that the books would never have acquired the unique position they came to have in the religious life of the nation, but for that highly-trained spiritual discernment, the very genius of the Jewish people, which enabled men to see in them that something which we speak of as inspiration. That perception of their value came first; and then, with the passage of time, the increased use of the books and the growing familiarity with their contents, came to invest them with a powerful authority in religious matters, such as appealed to every conscience; until, at last, in their separateness, they acquired a peculiar degree of sanctity, to which no other writings could pretend. And so the process of canonisation was completed. But it is time to return to a discussion of this process in more detail.

19. Almost every people in a primitive stage of civilisation is possessed of its folk-songs and

Ancient songs

folk-lore, which have accumulated through the centuries, nobody knows how, and which contain in them elements that, could we trace them, would take

us back to a hoar antiquity. It is frequently such things
as these which first get committed to writing, when
that art makes its appearance. Thus we shall not be
surprised to find that some of the oldest pieces of
literature in the Bible are certain songs, or portions of
songs. And we notice at once that these are imbued
with a certain religious spirit; for they speak of the
great exploits of the national heroes, and of the ways
in which God, by their means, exhibited His protective
care for His people. We have, to cite a few specimens,
'The Song of Moses' (Ex. xv. 1—18), 'The Song of
Victory' (Num. xxi. 27—30), 'The Song of Deborah'
(Jud. v. 2—31), and 'The Dirge of David' (2 Sam. i.
19—27).

We hear, in these days, of antiquaries who busy themselves in collecting, mainly from illiterate
old people, folk-songs which are only re-
tained in the memories of a few and have thus come
near to being lost, and then reducing them to writing.
And it is at least a possibility that the occasion on
which many of these old Hebrew songs were first written
down, was when they were collected from a sense of their
religious value, and with a view to giving them a wider
publicity. We have mention of at any rate two such
early written collections; 'The Book of the Wars of
the Lord' (Num. xxi. 14), and 'The Book of Jasher'
(Josh. x. 13: 2 Sam. i. 18). And in this connection we
may notice, what we have already alluded to, that in
such collections it was customary to bring together a
number of anonymous pieces under the name of some one
great man, of whom tradition said that he wrote songs.
In this way, for instance, the songs of Deut. xxxii,
xxxiii, were attributed to Moses, though there are

features in them which show that they were compositions belonging to a later date than his. Fragments from such written collections of songs were freely transcribed by the authors of the main sources of which our books are composed.

20. One of the greatest problems with which our Indian administrators have had to deal has been that which is known as customary law. Their intention has been, not to thrust upon our Indian fellow-subjects a mass of English law which they could not be expected to understand, and which would not suit their conditions of life; but, rather, to interpret and administer the existing native law equably and fairly. But this involved an immensely difficult study; partly because the law differed in different districts and amongst different tribes; and still more because it only existed as a matter of custom, a usage handed down by word of mouth from generation to generation; and it was necessary to collect, codify, and put into writing this customary law. The early Hebrews were, of course, in a very similar position to the less advanced Indian peoples of to-day. Originally all their law was a matter of custom; and this would have differed to some extent in their different tribes; and it would have undergone some changes corresponding to the change in the conditions of their life. For instance, the whole body of law suitable to a people peaceably settled, and busied with agricultural operations, would not have been applicable to the same people during an earlier phase in their history, when they were leading a nomadic life in the deserts, hunting for their food. It is necessary to carry this in mind if we are to understand the legal systems we find in the Old Testament.

Customary Law.

21. There can be no doubt that much of the
Hebrew law is of an immense antiquity.
The Hebrews were, as we have noticed,
but a small branch of the great Semitic people. As
such, they naturally shared with their fellows a vast
mass of social custom and religious rites, whose authority
was unquestioned and was implicitly obeyed. These
things had come down to them from bygone ages ; their
origin was quite unknown; but they were handed on
by habit and training, and in some measure by word
of mouth, when these laws came to be expressed in a
set form of words. It is a characteristic of primitive
races that their whole law is built upon a religious
foundation ; there is no clear distinction between the
laws which are concerned with the worship of their
god, those which relate to the operations of agriculture,
or those which have to do with questions of morality ;
for it was held that the whole life of a tribe was bound
up with that of its god, who was equally active in the
court of law, the cornfield, the temple, or the family
hearth. Thus we may say that the Hebrews differed
from their neighbours, in respect of their laws, only as
their religion, the God whom they worshipped, differed.
A study of other Semitic races, therefore, both helps
us to see what were the sources from which the Hebrew
customs and rites were derived, to grasp how much they
had in common with other tribes, and to understand the
meaning of what is often so strange to us at the present
day. For instance, the discovery of the 'Code of
Ḥammurabi' (possibly the King Amraphel of Gen. xiv. 1),
a Babylonian production which is dated circ. 2000 B.C.,
has made us see that much of the Hebrew social law
was very much older than the days of Moses. And a

comparison with other sources of information enables us to trace back to more primitive times the origin of a priesthood, the institution of the prophet, the rite of circumcision, the use of the sabbath, a great deal of the sacrificial system and the religious symbolism which characterised the worship of the Temple, the lofty conception, it may be, of an ethical monotheism, and possibly even the sacred name, if not the attributes, of Yahweh Himself.

22. But it may reasonably be asked, 'What, then, becomes of the law-giving on Sinai?' Any answer to this question must, at the present, be largely conjectural. Legend has been very busy about that great event, which was practically the birthday of the Hebrew people; and probably it is impossible that we shall ever be able to reconstruct what actually took place then and there. But of this we may feel assured, that what lies behind the vast accretion of legend is a fact of great historical importance. It seems clear that Yahweh was closely associated with the region, or mountain, of Sinai; and, judging from the recorded mode of His manifestation, it may be that He was originally a thunder-god. In that case the stones enshrined in the ark, which appears to have been a very ancient feature in Yahwehism, may have been meteorites. If some few only of the Hebrews were resident in Egypt, it is possible that Sinai witnessed their amalgamation with other of their kinsmen, dwelling around Sinai; and that this amalgamation took the form of a blood-covenant, and the adoption by the Egyptian Hebrews, whose god was represented by a calf, of the Sinaitic god Yahweh, and the ritual customs and laws connected with His worship. If that were so, then it

Significance of Sinai.

becomes easier to perceive what was the work of Moses
as a law-giver, and what the significance of the law-
giving.   For we may surmise that Sinai did not witness
the promulgation of a novel code of laws, but rather
the blending of two bodies of customary laws already
in existence, belonging to two groups of the Hebrew
people, under the authority of the god Yahweh. Perhaps
we may go so far as to say, that at that time, by virtue
of this covenant with the Yahweh worshippers, the whole
body of law became, in the estimation of the people,
Divine, stamped with the sanction and authority of
Yahweh Himself. Thenceforward, perhaps, the whole
legal code possessed a new sanctity, and was impressed
with a special religious feeling. This is all, of course,
somewhat speculative; but it probably indicates the sort
of direction in which an answer must be looked for.

23.   But the Sinaitic code was not a rigid system,
such as could never, in any respect or in
any circumstances, be altered. In the earlier
books of the Old Testament we discover
two versions of the Decalogue, which are not harmonious;
we find parallel laws on the same matters, which do not
agree ; we perceive different modes of treatment of the
body of law in general.   And, taking these facts into
account, we realise that, with the process of time, the
Hebrews expanded and modified their laws, to suit the
varying conditions of their life as they passed from one
stage of civilisation to another, and to make them
correspond with their religious conceptions as these
deepened and became more spiritual.   Moreover, we
find, as we should expect, that in the Old Testament
we actually possess different collections of laws, dating
from different periods, and reflecting different phases in

Subsequent
legal
developments.

the people's history. But it is true to say that, while
the laws underwent a certain change, their underlying
spirit, their religious motive and sanction, always remained the same. Thus the Jews could look back
to Moses as their great law-giver with considerable
historical justification; and when they came to call the
whole legal system of the Pentateuch 'The Law of
Moses,' there was at least this in favour of their
judgment—not that Moses either wrote or gave what
we find in the Scriptural books, but that all contained
in them is conceived on the same lines, and in the same
religious spirit, as Moses inculcated. It is all of it, that
is to say, a true development of his teaching.

24. Here we may stay to examine, very briefly,
what is meant by the development to which
the books of the Old Testament bear
witness. We spoke above, in passing, of
an ethical monotheism as being characteristic of the
later Jewish faith; and this reminds us that the growth
of religious conceptions and moral ideas always went
hand in hand. The prophets were the embodiment of
the national conscience; always in advance of the moral
ideas of their people, they enunciated great principles of
righteousness, of which they would have their hearers
perceive the force. And they thus spoke as being the
inspired mouth-pieces of God Himself; they claimed to
utter God's word, to declare the Divine mind to men.
In general, it may be said that the prophet was in
conflict with the priest; for the tendency of the priesthood was to lay all the emphasis upon the outward
forms of religion, and to claim that God would be
satisfied with a proper performance of the rituals of
sacrifice and purification. This was to divest religion of

*Development,
religious
and moral.*

all moral significance; and it opened the door to superstition and magic. Against this tendency the prophet
rebelled; and, in his protest that God demanded of man,
before all else, an upright character and an acknowledgement of the duties of humanity, he, in his turn,
tended towards the opposite extreme, and to the over-
depreciation of the value of religious forms and symbols
(cp. e.g. Amos v. 21—27). Nevertheless it was the
prophet to whom was due the development of Hebrew
theology. In the earliest days, doubtless, the jealousies
and power of a priesthood may have had something to
do with the increasing range of the worship of a
particular divinity; as had also the growing prosperity
and the conquests of the tribe whose divinity he was.
But when once a god had attained the established
position of a national deity, then it was the prophet
who paved the way to an advance in theological doctrine.
When he declared that moral conduct was the will of
God, it would have been quickly perceived that the
righteousness of man implied a still more exalted
righteousness in God; that He could only demand
holiness in man, because He was Himself holy. But
this conception was fertile of much else. If God was
holy, and not only expected righteousness of man, but
also punished man's evil-doing; then, by easy stages, it
would have been perceived that an almost infinite gulf
in the matter of holiness separated God and man; and
that, while God was morally perfect, man must be a
sinner; and thus there would have arisen a sense of
guilt, the need of penitence, and so forth. But, beside
this, a morally perfect God, contrasted with the divinities
of neighbouring peoples, would have stood, first in a
position of supremacy, and then in isolation; first it

would have appeared that He was exalted above every other god, and then that the other gods were no gods, and that He was God alone. And that, again, would have led to a further step ; for the only God could not be, by any possibility, a mere tribal deity, but must assuredly be the God of all the earth, as universal in His sway as He was supreme in His holiness. And, this position once attained, there could be no limitation to the development of the moral ideas to which it would give rise. Now this is descriptive of the sort of growth, in religion and morality, which we can actually trace in the writings of the Old Testament. There is a vast difference between the conception implied in Jacob's words, 'Surely Yahweh is in this place; and I knew it not' (Gen. xxviii. 16^b), and those of the unknown prophet, 'I will also give thee for a light to the Gentiles, that my salvation may be unto the end of the earth' (Is. xlix. 6^b). Similarly, to take a single illustration, the distance is enormous which separates such an incident as the slaughter of seven of Saul's sons (described in 2 Sam. xxi. 1—9), whom the Gibeonites 'hanged...in the mountain *before the Lord*,' and Ezekiel's 'the soul that sinneth, it shall die' (cp. Ez. xviii. 1—4).

25. But we must return from this digression to notice who were the guardians of the Law.

Law the province of the Priests.

If the social order of a primitive people like the Hebrews rested upon a religious foundation, we can readily understand why it was that the priesthood played so important a part in the national life. The priests not only directed the worship of God ; they were also the judges of the people, the guardians and executors of the Law. They were responsible, not only for the regulations respecting the rites of sacrifice

and the functions of the priesthood, but also for all civil
law, since that was also regarded as being, in a sense,
religious. Thus, during all the time that the laws were
subject, from generation to generation, to oral delivery,
it was the priests who knew and applied the Law; and
when the people went to them for judgment, it was
generally recognised that their verdicts must be accepted
as the inspired oracles of God. Moreover, the rulings
of the priest-judges in particular cases certainly created
precedents, which attained the force of law in future
times. It is possible that the earliest form of written
and codified law may have been a collection made by
the priests for their own use and guidance.

26. In the principal sources of our present books
Collection of   we notice distinct collections of laws, dating
Laws.   from different periods, which have either
been incorporated into the narrative, or around which an
historical setting has been built up. If we study with
care the 'Book of the Covenant,' to which we have
already alluded, we shall discover it to be a code of laws
suitable to a very primitive condition of society. It is a
collection rather loosely put together, and not by any
means exhaustive; and it is possible that one of the
authors of E (in which document it is found) may have
seen an official collection, from which he compiled this
by memory. The 'Law of Holiness' differs, mainly in
its subject-matter, from the 'Book of the Covenant';
and, though its style and language point to its being a
later production, there can be no doubt that a great part
of the laws it contains are of a considerable antiquity.
The 'Kernel of Deuteronomy' was, as we have seen, an
earlier collection than the 'Law of Holiness'; but both
of them, in all probability, were compiled from previous

collections. The distinctive mark of Deuteronomy is, that the laws are not barely stated but interpreted, and backed by moral exhortations. This suits very well the extraordinary effect it is said to have produced, if we are inclined to identify it with the law-book discovered in the Temple, and read before Josiah and his court. The remainder of the legislation in the 'Priestly Code' is a later collection, but undoubtedly contains much ancient material. In fact, in all these different levels of legal enactments we are able to see at work a continuous process of expansion and expurgation; an attempt to create a system of law that should at once preserve the oldest elements which still had their value, put into an authoritative form customs which actually obtained, and create further regulations to meet the requirements of a new generation. And, throughout, we observe the same religious genius at work, and the same loyalty to the fundamental principles of Divine revelation.

27. We have noticed that the early poetry and legal codes of the Hebrews are incorporated in historical narratives, or have had an historical framework constructed on purpose to carry them. We have also noticed that the four principal narratives, which our literary analysis enables us to detect, carry us through all the historical books down to the end of Kings. We have said something of Hebrew songs and Hebrew laws; it now remains for us to give some attention to Hebrew history. And the first thing we have to note about the historical writings of the Old Testament is, that they are not history in the sense we accord to that term at the present day. They are history written with a purpose; that purpose being a religious one. Throughout, the

Historical Narratives.

History with a purpose.

authors or editors have kept one principal aim steadily in view; to make clear to their readers that the hand of their God has been ever busy in shaping their national progress and destinies. And so they have not attempted to record in full all the material with which they might have provided us; but, rather, they have judiciously selected the events which, in their opinion, were best calculated to point the morals upon which they insisted. For the same reason they have introduced such characters into their drama as were most suited to illustrate these religious motives; and they pass judgments upon persons, events and policies, such as their religious principles dictate. Moreover, the strife of religious parties, with which we are not unfamiliar in our own day, and of which we hear a great deal in New Testament times, undoubtedly existed amongst the ancient Hebrews; with the natural result that we have histories written from different points of view. Not, indeed, that the religious judgment is ever in abeyance; but that, for example, an historical character, whose views were those of one party, may be seen to suffer at the hands of an historian of another.

28. These considerations, taken in connection with a faulty system of chronology, should put us on our guard when we attempt to form an opinion of how certain historical events actually transpired, and what were the political and other motives underlying a whole sequence of such events. For the Hebrew ideas of chronology were very rudimentary and inexact. Not only had they no universal era, similar to our Christian era; but, until the times of the Maccabees, they had not even a national era, like that of Rome. Thus most of the attempts, found in the Old Testament,

Chronology.

to date events, are not founded upon tradition or careful historical investigation, but are merely a late, and rough and ready, guess-work. In order to establish the correct date of any particular event, or to estimate the chronological relations of events, we are therefore driven to rely upon external evidence; evidence which is provided, to some extent, by the Egyptian King-lists, but in larger measure by the Assyrian lists, whose accuracy is beyond dispute. But to the matter of chronology we propose to return later; and here it must suffice to say that the earliest date we can at present fix with any accuracy in Hebrew history, is the defeat of Ahab (after his alliance with Benhadad, cp. 1 Kings xx. 34) by Shalmaneser II at Qarqar, in the year 854 B.C. Behind that all is, as yet, purely conjectural.

29. The Hebrews were like every other nation of antiquity, boasting any records whatever of their early history, in possessing traditions which may roughly be classified as mythology, legend, and history proper. It is unnecessary to do more than to point to Greece or Scandinavia, in order to illustrate the meaning of this classification. It is not always easy to draw the line, and to tell, for instance, where legend ends and history begins; but a rough distinction between the two is easily discernible.

Threefold distinction.

The narratives of the creation of the world, the origin of the first man, the entry of sin into the world by way of the fall, the great flood and the ark, and the tower of Babel, are all of them clearly mythological, which is to say imaginative. Originally they belonged to the common stock of Semitic fables, and represent primitive man's crude attempts to explain the great problems which met him

(i.) Mythology.

in the world of nature and in human life. Some of these stories are world-wide in their provenance, being found amongst barbarous tribes from North America to Ceylon, from New Zealand to Somaliland. But the form which approximates most nearly to the Hebrew version is the ancient Babylonian. And yet the difference between the two is very marked. In the Babylonian stories we find the most extravagant polytheistic ideas, and much else that offends our religious and moral sense ; but in the Hebrew account most of this is purged away, and the stories themselves have become the beautiful and majestic vehicles for conveying the highest spiritual truth. It is possible that, in the case of the Priestly Code, some of this purification may have been effected by Zoroastrianism, and that the Jews already found their mythology in the way of becoming elevated for them during the Persian period. But the fact remains that the stories assumed their final shape in Hebrew hands, and are the work of their religious instinct. Thus we may learn that God has chosen to reveal Himself to men through these old-world allegories ; just as Jesus, at a much later date, chose to disclose the secrets of His Kingdom by the means of parables.

From the sphere of mythology we pass to that of legend. If we bear in mind that the (ii.) **Legend.** traditions embodied, for example, in the stories of the patriarchs, must have been handed down by word of mouth for several hundreds of years before ever they came to be recorded in writing, we shall hardly expect them to contain accurate historical information. They correspond, indeed, with the heroic periods of other ancient peoples ; tales which were told about the camp fires by night, and which grew in the telling, to account for the veneration in which the tribal ancestors were held, or to chain the imagination by the recital of the glorious deeds of a golden past. But traditions of this sort, however much they may gather to themselves in the course of ages, do not arise without a reason,—without, that is to say, some solid basis in fact. Mythological inventions will frequently have grown out of astronomical phenomena, owing to the tendency of the primitive mind to personify the heavenly bodies; but behind legend there must usually lie historical data. Therefore it is very probable that an Abraham, an Isaac and a Jacob, do actually represent real personages who had an importance for religious history; a Moses almost certainly does so. On the other hand, an Esau or a Joseph may merely stand for certain tribes with a similar designation, whose very existence as a tribe was forgotten; and, in the case of Joseph, it is possible that his story owes something to an old Egyptian tale. A Samson, again, is probably an historical character almost wholly obscured by the creations of an imaginative fancy. A study of similar legendary materials belonging to other races teaches us to anticipate that the migrations, alliances and exploits of tribes and heroes, as they were retold from generation to generation, would have become increasingly the subjects of imaginative treatment; and that noteworthy stories, possessing no particular home of their own, would have become attached to famous names; and, again, that the whole cycle of narratives would have been worked up by the art of the narrator to suit the taste of his audience. This is all parallel, for instance, to the history of the legends of King Arthur. But though we may be able to see how these legends have grown, it must remain very largely a matter of conjecture, to determine what of historical foundation belongs to each of them in particular. And, as was the case with the Hebrew mythology, so here again we are brought to acknowledge and admire the profound religious force and moral beauty of these legendary tales, which have proved themselves capable of conveying the highest spiritual teaching, and therefore the very revelation of God Himself.

But here we should utter a word of apology. The A defence of use of the terms 'mythology' and 'legend,' the terms as descriptive of a great deal of the material 'mythology' and 'legend.' contained in these ancient narratives, should cause no offence to our religious feeling. If we are prepared to see God revealing Himself to man progressively and by human means, so that the whole process of revelation is capable of historical study ; then we should rather expect that the writings containing that revelation will not have been originally composed with a full consciousness of the truth they convey. It was, we should anticipate, because they were seen to possess religious value that they were treasured ; and it was because men's spiritual discernment became keener, with the fuller revelation of later days, that the narratives were purified of the features which that discernment condemned. It is our part, not to quarrel with the method by which God chose to reveal Himself, but to wonder at the marvellous fertility in the devices He employed to make Himself known, and to observe with awe the extraordinary magnitude and intricacy of the processes which we must include under the name of Inspiration. The value of a thing is not to be estimated by its origin ; and religious truth does not suffer even if we should deem its mode of entry into the world somewhat disreputable.

Realising the inestimable worth of what we possess, however, we should do wisely to study its human parentage as a supreme exhibition of the wisdom and the goodness of God. A generation ago, the large majority of religious people were found to scout a simian ancestry of man, as derogatory to human dignity and to God's character. That view has now almost disappeared; and, in the same way, there will presently disappear the objection to the statement that God's self-revelation was first made through the medium of mythological and legendary tales.

The narratives of the settlement of the Hebrews in (iii.) History Canaan, and of the period of the Judges, proper. undoubtedly contain a great deal of valuable historical material; but, since the events recorded were only committed to writing after the lapse of a considerable interval of time, the accounts we possess must be very carefully sifted in order that the amount of historical truth they contain may be extracted from them. The year 1887 saw the discovery, at Tel el-Amarna in Egypt, of a number of tablets inscribed in the Babylonian cuneiform script. They proved to contain a correspondence, which passed between certain governors and kings in Canaan and Egyptian officials, written a little previously to the Hebrew invasion of Palestine, about the year 1500 B.C. These have recently been supplemented by a quantity of similar tablets, belonging to the same period, found in the ruins at Boghaz-keui, the site of the capital of the ancient Hittite empire. Together, these tablets conclusively prove that, at the time when the Hebrew tribes were effecting an entrance to Canaan, the land was an Egyptian province penetrated throughout by Babylonian culture. The

total, or almost total, absence of any mention of the
Hebrews on Egyptian monuments of the period, leads
us to suspect that only a small portion of the people, one
or two tribes perhaps, were actually resident in Egypt.
It is indeed possible that, as some scholars think, the
whole episode has grown out of a confusion between
Mizraim, the Hebrew name for Egypt, and a North
Arabian kingdom of Mizrim, adjoining the southern
district of Palestine known as the Negeb.   But a discussion of this view, together with the allied problem
of the association of the Hebrew clans with the Jerahmeelites, who may have been of North Arabian origin,
would involve too close a survey of critical arguments to
be attempted here.   Before the settlement in Palestine
the history of the Hebrews is lost in obscurity ; and
scholarship can, at the most, lift a corner of the veil,
here and there, to enable us to catch a glimpse of what
was transpiring in those prehistoric days.   The actual
invasion of Canaan was clearly a very gradual process,
carried out by successive waves which subsequently
became united.   This view is supported by the fragmentary information supplied by the Scriptural documents
themselves ; for the period of the Judges presents us
with a picture of how the different tribes were banded
together under a common leader, first here and then
there, in the face of a common enemy ; and it is not
until some while after the establishment of the monarchy
that the people were finally coalesced into a nation and
consolidated in an organised kingdom.

And thus it is that, not until we reach the days of
Saul and David do we really feel ourselves
to be upon solid ground.   It is true that
even in these later narratives much of a

Contemporary
annals, and
historical
writings.

legendary character has been interwoven ; but the important point to notice is that, with the monarchy, we begin to deal less with oral tradition, and for the first time we come in touch with written documents of a more or less contemporary character. Moreover, at this period we are able, to some extent, to check the statements of Hebrew historians by reference to Assyrian inscriptions. The earliest written records were, doubtless, the royal annals which were kept by a scribe attached to the court; and they would have dealt with the bare facts of military operations, victories and defeats, foreign alliances, the royal succession, court intrigues, taxation, and the national resources. These would have been collected from time to time by historians of the prophetical schools, whose motive was always a religious one, and who were naturally unable to discriminate between such sources of information and the legendary and mythological material upon which they wove their story. Thus there would have been produced the early historical books, such as 'The Book of the Acts of Solomon' and 'The Book of the Chronicles of the Kings of Judah,' of which our existing historical documents made extensive use, when they in their turn, during the great period of literary activity which the Babylonian exile saw, came to be compiled.

30. We have, so far, been engaged in sketching the preliminary stages in the formation of a Canon of Scripture. These were, in the main, a gradual selection of a mass of varied material, which either possessed, or was then invested with, a peculiar religious character. But, up to the close of the exile, with the solitary exception of the book reported to have been discovered in the reign of Josiah, there is no

The beginning of a Canon.

hint of any recognition of any one book, or collection of books, possessing that sanctity which would entitle it to a special reverence. With the return from the exile, however, the first step in this direction was taken.

Some hundred and thirty years before the birth of our Lord the Jews had already come to speak of their Scriptures as a threefold collection. They referred to them as 'The Law (Torah), the Prophets (Nebhiim), and the Writings (Kethubhim—or, in the Greek, Hagiographa).' So we find it stated in the Prologue to Ecclesiasticus, which was written at about the date mentioned above; and it is of interest to observe that the Hebrew Bible is still arranged after this order. The Nebhiim were further divided into 'the former and the latter Prophets'; a distinction which applies, not to the times of their production, but to the positions they held in the sacred collection. The Torah embraced the five books, Genesis to Deuteronomy. The former Prophets included Joshua and Judges, Samuel and Kings; and, with regard to the last two books, we should notice that they had not then been severally split into two portions. The latter Prophets included Isaiah, Jeremiah, Ezekiel, and the Twelve minor prophets which together formed a single book. And to the Hagiographa belonged the Psalms, Proverbs, Job, the Five Megilloth, Daniel, and (what was then a single continuous work) Chronicles-Ezra-Nehemiah. This threefold division, and the fact that the Jews accorded different degrees of reverence to each collection, in an ascending scale from the Hagiographa to the Torah, helps us very materially in tracing the history of the Canon; for undoubtedly it has an historical significance, and marks three separate steps in the process

Torah, Nebhiim, and Kethubhim.

which finally resulted in the Old Testament as we possess it.

31. It was, probably, in the year 398 B.C. that Ezra promulgated the Law at Jerusalem to the returned exiles. In all probability, what he then did was to make known the legal material in the newly formed Priestly Code, which he brought with him from Babylonia. As we have already noticed, the document P was united with the other sources JED, which were already combined, at some time immediately precedent or subsequent to the year of Ezra's proclamation. It would have been during this process of combination that the material was cut up into the separate books we now possess; for some division would have been necessary, owing to the fact that skin rolls were employed for the purpose of writing, and these would have had a certain limit as regards their length. Following shortly upon this, and again as a natural consequence, the remainders of the documents, which went to the composition of the 'former prophets,' were separated from the earlier portions, and the five books, Genesis, Exodus, Leviticus, Numbers and Deuteronomy, now stood alone as constituting the Torah. For the first and most important business of the returned exiles was of necessity the reconstruction and organisation of their whole civil and religious life, which had fallen to pieces during the captivity. Since the Jewish people was now a subject state, placed under the governorship of a nominee of the Persian king, that reconstruction tended more and more in the direction of the foundation of a religious community, a Church; for what national unity and independence they had was bound up with, and rested upon, their religious faith. Therefore their chief

Torah.

requirement was a clear expression of their ritual and ecclesiastical law. The historical books would, in the first instance, have possessed little practical value, in their eyes, in comparison with the collections of the Law; and, while the 'former prophets' were temporarily neglected, the Torah very soon advanced to a position of paramount authority and sanctity, as the expression of the Divine will through the agency of Moses. Now, though the Samaritans were excluded, by Nehemiah and his successor Ezra, from all participation in the worship of Yahweh at Jerusalem, this compulsory schism did not deprive them of their allegiance to the God of the Hebrews. They quickly developed their rival exposition of the faith, on Mount Gerizim, and they translated the whole of the existing Canon of Scripture into the Samaritan language. It is interesting, in this connection, to observe that the Samaritan Scriptures at no subsequent time exceeded the limits of the Torah. It is, at present, impossible to say exactly when this version was made; but it was probably not long after the year 397 B.C. And, if that is so, the Samaritan Pentateuch is evidence of the completion of the Torah, in the form in which we have it, by the early years of the fourth century before Christ. This, then, was the first step in the process of the formation of the Old Testament Canon.

It is worth noticing an important consequence following upon this step; a consequence which is significant of what was to follow. Hitherto the Law had remained in the hands of the priests, to preserve, to formulate and to administer. But now, by the authoritative publication of the whole mass of the Law, the Word of God was taken, for the first time, out of the hands of the priests, and placed in those of the people. Henceforward the priests

were no longer the inspired repositories of the oracles of
God, the law-givers and judges; for now all who could
read were able to know the law for themselves. There
remained but the interpretation of it to individual cases
and on particular occasions; and this became the special
work of a newly-formed body of men who came into
existence during the exile,—the Scribes; of whom Ezra
was the chief representative. Hence the important position Ezra came to occupy in Jewish tradition, as being,
after Moses, the great fountain-head of the Jewish Law.

32. The Nebhiim, we have seen, included not only
the prophetical writings proper, but also
the four chief historical books. Why these
historical writings came to be classed as
'prophetical' needs a word of explanation. We have
already noticed that a great deal of the material of these
books originally formed part of the documents from
which the books of the Pentateuch were compiled. We
have also noticed that the Pentateuch was given its final
shape by lopping off all that followed upon Deuteronomy; for the twofold reason that the canonisation of
the Law was the matter then in hand, and that the
Law was felt to be complete with the recorded death of
Moses the Law-giver. But we can understand that,
with the lapse of time, a certain sense of dissatisfaction
would have been entertained at the Torah being allowed
to stand in that truncated form. It would have been
remembered that the Law itself was largely indebted to
the prophets for its existence, since at all times a law-
giver must have been an inspired person. It would have
been realised that the recorded history of the Hebrew
people was a living illustration of the gradual growth
and recognition of the Law, and therefore its best

Nebhiim.
(i.) The Former
Prophets.

interpreter in practice. It is perhaps true to say that much of the historical writing produced was the actual work of the prophetical schools. But, above these considerations, there would doubtless have arisen the feeling that in the historical books, as well as in those which were strictly prophetical, the main interest centres round the work of the prophets themselves. The prevailing opinion was to the effect that all Divine revelation was made through the medium of the prophet, whose business it was to declare the mind of God to his generation. And, indeed, a study of the extant teaching of that wonderful succession of inspired men shows the prophetic institution amongst the Hebrews to have been an unique phenomenon in the whole range of religious history and experience. But now the long chain of prophecy, if it had not altogether ceased, was waxing faint and showing signs of decay. No longer could the living voice of God, speaking by a human mouth-piece, be heard amongst the people with its accustomed vigour and force. The fathers had slain the prophets; and the children had come to reverence them only when the institution was already moribund. Moreover, the actual writing of the Law had already stereotyped it, and was like to produce a conventional obedience which might easily sap the religious life of all vitality and inspiration. There was, therefore, all the more need to rescue and conserve, not alone the remains of the vivid teaching of the great men of old, who at last, after centuries of opposition and misunderstanding, had come to their own; but also the historical writings which pictured them at work, and which were so full of dire warning, by reason of the little success they had been permitted to achieve in their day. Thus the same causes which would have operated to preserve the actual books of prophecy would also have contributed to raise in the popular estimation, as being themselves truly prophetical, those historical works in which the finger of God was to be so clearly seen at work in the history of His people.

Of the 'latter' prophets it is unnecessary to speak **(ii.) The Latter Prophets.** here at any length. Isaiah we have already discussed; but it remains to give a brief account of the authorship, dates and literary analysis **(a) Jeremiah.** of the remaining prophetical works. Jeremiah's work fell during that stormy period which saw the downfall of the Kingdom of Judah, and the beginning of the captivity. His prophecies were some of them uttered by word of mouth, while others saw the light for the first time in literary form. A large portion of them was given to the world in the prophet's native country; but a part is to be dated from his exile in Egypt. The great bulk of the work which goes by his name is, undoubtedly, authentic. The story related in Jer. xxxvi may probably be taken for a true description of the genesis of the first two editions of the nucleus of our present book; and Jer. xxx. 1 points to the addition of an appendix to the original work. We gather that Jeremiah did not himself commit his prophecies to writing, but dictated them to Baruch; to whom we should probably ascribe the biographical material which the book contains, and a great deal of prophecy which he may have worked up from memory, or from notes taken at the time of its utterance. A comparison of the text, as it exists in the Hebrew, with the LXX version, exhibits a very marked difference between the two. This difference consists, mainly, in the transpositions of the order of the prophecies, and in the large omissions, which are the characteristic of the LXX version. It is probable that there may have existed, in Egypt and in Palestine, two Hebrew recensions of the book, a longer and a shorter; and that the LXX translation was made from the shorter, while our Hebrew Massoretic text has preserved for us the longer, with its many editorial additions. The fact that there are these additions, and the dependence upon Kings which the book reveals in certain places, point to its having reached its present form at some time subsequent to the return from the exile.

The activity of Ezekiel as a prophet fell in the first half of the Babylonian captivity. The book which bears his name, except for a few passages (which may however be dislocations rather than interpolations), appears to be the work of a single mind, and is doubtless genuine throughout. In that case its composition would have occupied the prophet's last years, and may approximately be dated in 570 B.C. A great part of the book is concerned with matter which clearly was given to the public for the first time in a literary form. Ezekiel seems to have been the prime mover in the development of that ecclesiastical polity, which was later to gain its practical realisation at the hands of Ezra. In the passage xliii. 18—xlv. 8 the author is plainly parting company with the Deuteronomic Law, when he exalts the house of Zadok at the expense of the majority of the Levites; and the whole section xl—xlviii is closely related to the 'Law of Holiness.' Thus the later Priestly Code is associated with the name of Ezekiel; and it may have been that connection, and a reflection of the sanctity attaching to

(β) Ezekiel.

the Code, which preserved Ezekiel's book from the inclusion of editorial additions.

We are dependent entirely upon their internal historical evidence for dating the twelve books which, on account of their brevity, are usually known as the Minor Prophets.

(γ) Book of the Twelve Prophets.

It seems that when they were admitted to the Canon of the Old Testament they already formed, and were counted as, a single book. But that implies that they were a collection of writings, belonging to very different periods, which was made by a number of hands rather than by a single editor; and that the process of collecting them was spread over a long period of time. Many of these writings contain only fragments of the prophetic utterances of the men to whom they are ascribed; some embrace stray prophecies of unknown authorship; all of them betray the hand of the editor, and in some cases this amounts to considerable interpolation; and while the literary form is often to be ascribed to the prophet himself, we must frequently attribute it to the diligence of his disciples. We will here review them in what, according to the opinion of some scholars, is their chronological order. Amos has the distinction of being the first Hebrew prophet whose teaching has been recorded; and if we may take it that his memoirs and sayings were collected soon after his death, then the first appearance of his book may be dated about 750 B.C. Hosea, who was his younger contemporary, carried on his mission some twenty years later; and we may put the original of his work about 730 B.C. With regard to this book, one of the most interesting problems that arises is whether we are to regard the first three chapters as biographical or purely allegorical. Micah was the

B. 6

contemporary of Isaiah, and was therefore active in the closing years of the eighth century. Thus we may place his book about the year 690 B.C. Zephaniah prophesied in the days of Josiah, but apparently his recorded words were spoken previous to that king's reforming movement, which he may have contributed to inspire. Thus we may, perhaps, date his book about 625 B.C. Nahum, who must have been his contemporary, probably prophesied within a few years of the destruction of Nineveh, which he predicts; and the year 610 B.C. may have seen the production of his work. Habakkuk, who was contemporary with the first portion of Jeremiah's ministry, preached during the closing years of the seventh century; and his book probably saw the light before the destruction of Jerusalem in 586 B.C. Obadiah prophesied in Judah during the first stage of the exile; and his work may have synchronised with that of Ezekiel, in or about the year 570 B.C. It is worth noticing that the first nine verses of his short book are an adaptation of a much older, but anonymous, prophecy. Haggai is the earliest of the prophets of the returned exiles; and the editor dates his prophecies exactly in the year 520 B.C. The book known by the name of Zechariah falls into two divisions, which belong to very different dates. The second part, which is anonymous, probably owed its junction to the genuine book of Zechariah to the accident of propinquity. Zechariah himself was contemporary with Haggai; and his prophecies, which are included in chapters i—viii, are exactly dated in the years 520—518 B.C. In him we discover the earliest appearance, but for Ezekiel, of distinct apocalyptic, or visionary, teaching. The book known as 'Malachi' is really anonymous; for the word, which occurs in the introductory verse, simply means 'my messenger.' This unknown prophet appears to have done work which was preparatory to the reforms introduced by Nehemiah; and we may therefore place his book about 450 B.C. Joel is one of the latest prophets, and was probably active towards the close of the Persian period. His book may possibly be given to somewhere about the year 370 B.C. Jonah, the son of Amittai, prophesied in the reign of Jeroboam II; but the book which goes by his name is an allegory, composed during the Greek period, perhaps about the year 280 B.C. Thus the latest prophetic writing to be included in the collection was the anonymous Zechariah ix—xiv, which may even come down so far as the year 250 B.C.

The process by which all these writings, former prophets and latter prophets alike, came to be embraced within the Canon of Scripture cannot be described otherwise than conjecturally. But the Synagogue was probably largely instrumental in gaining them that recognition. That is to say that, side by side with a general and increasing interest in this range of literature, there would have grown up the custom of reading portions of the 'Prophets' in the course of the services, as being explanatory and illustrative of the passages prescribed to be read from the Torah. It is impossible to say definitely, in the present state of our information, when the prophetical books reached their final form, and received their last editorial revision; but they must have been substantially as we now have them previous to their translation into Greek, somewhere about the year 200 B.C. It is very probable that the gradual acceptance of the Nebhiim, to take rank beside the Torah as Scripture, would have occupied about the space of a century, beginning some three hundred, and

Importance of Synagogue.

6—2

ending some two hundred years before Christ. Thus we mark the second chief step in the process of the formation of the Hebrew Canon.

33. With regard to the remaining books of the Old Testament, which were grouped together as the Kethubhim or Hagiographa, we notice, in the first place, that many of them are of a very different type of literature from anything that had previously gained admittance to the Canon. That they had not been included with the Nebhiim is undeniably due to the fact that they had not yet obtained the same religious currency; in other words, they had not been read, as were the Law and the Prophets, in the synagogues.

Kethubhim.

The books themselves were not, by any means, all of them more modern than the completed books of the Prophets, or even of the Law. The most important of them, the Psalms, while it may not have reached its final form until about 135 B.C., consists nevertheless of a number of separate collections which are of far earlier date. The titles of the various hymns are an indication of the sources from which the final compilation was made, namely the liturgical hymn-books of the different temple choirs. Some of these collections, the earliest of which may probably be dated in the times of Nehemiah, had had a religious use in the Temple services for many generations; but the individual songs which go to form these collections are clearly, many of them, far more ancient than the collections themselves. But, as separate collections, the Psalms had been, in the main, confined to the use and ministrations of Priests and Levites. It was with the introduction of the completed book into the Canon that they became public

(i.) Their various dates.

property, and entered into the religious life of the people as a devotional book of the highest order. The book of Proverbs is also a collection of collections, which may have reached its present form somewhere about the year 250 B.C. Two of these previous collections, chapters x. 1—xxii. 16 and xxv—xxix, were probably made before the exile; and all of them contain material which is of great age. The book as a whole is what it professes to be, a volume of practical commonsense. Job, a speculative poem of striking beauty, belongs in its completed form to the period shortly after the close of the exile; as does also the lovely little idyll Ruth; though the latter probably contains much older material. The internal evidence certainly points to an exilic date for Lamentations; but its style is against the ascription of it to Jeremiah. Ecclesiastes and the Song of Songs may both belong to somewhere about the year 200 B.C.; to which date we should also assign Esther. The inclusion of these three books in the Canon is a matter of literary curiosity; for Ecclesiastes is distinctly a sceptical production, the Song of Songs belongs to the class of amatory poems, and Esther, which nowhere contains any mention of God, is unhistorical and may be based upon a Babylonian myth. With regard to the three books Chronicles, Ezra and Nehemiah, a word of explanation is necessary. Originally they formed a single work, of which the component parts stood in the order in which we have them in our English Bible. But in the Hebrew Bible Ezra and Nehemiah stand before Chronicles; and this clearly indicates the order in which the books were received into the Canon. It is very probable that the portion Ezra-Nehemiah was lopped off from Chronicles and given a place in the Canon, to supply a need that had been felt; a need, that is, for a continuation of the historical narratives to the period beyond the exile, and covering the reconstruction of the Jewish state and church. Chronicles, which was largely based upon Kings and supplied but little new, or authentic, material, would only have been added after a great deal of hesitation. The internal indications point to the composition of the entire work somewhere between 300 and 250 B.C.; but, whereas the original matter of Chronicles must be received with some suspicion, the historical character of Ezra-Nehemiah is far more considerable; and it is probable that here the compiler was only revising an already existing work, based to a large extent, as we can see, upon contemporary authorities. But it appears very likely that he transposed the arrangement of the books, in the interest of Ezra, whom tradition ranked next to Moses; for the history of the period is far more intelligible if we date Ezra's first visit to Jerusalem after, and not before, the period of Nehemiah's activity. There remains only the book of Daniel, which appears to be the latest of all the Old Testament writings. The work makes no claim to be the composition of Daniel himself; for, on the one hand, the narrative section (i—vi) is in the third person, and, on the other hand, we know that it was a common literary device of apocalyptic writers to express their views through the medium of some great personage of the past. The first half of the book may be based upon tradition; but it is chronologically impossible that the hero can be identical with the Daniel of Ezekiel xiv. 14, xxviii. 3. Therefore we may suppose that the hero of the book is a creation of the imagination. The apocalyptic section contains four historical sketches, each of which ends with the persecution by Antiochus Epiphanes;

but since his death is still in the future, and here, as well
as in the vision of Nebuchadnezzar, the foundation of
the Kingdom of God is anticipated at the dissolution of
the Greek power, the book must probably be dated
previous to his death in 164 B.C., and subsequent to his
desecration of the Temple in 168 B.C. Further, if viii. 14
was written shortly before, or soon after, the reconsecra-
tion of the Temple, we may probably place the work
definitely in the year 165 B.C. And this conclusion is
supported by a variety of considerations; such as, the
relative ignorance of the Babylonian and Persian period
compared with the knowledge displayed of the times of
Antiochus; the absence of the book from the Nebhiim
in the Hebrew Canon, though that included such late
productions as Zachariah ix—xiv; and the absence of
all mention of Daniel previous to 165 B.C. (even in
Ecclesiasticus xliv—l, which may be dated about
200 B.C.), while subsequent to that date the influence of
the book is soon to be discovered—as in a portion of the
Sibylline Oracles, usually dated about 140 B.C. We
have already noticed that the whole section ii. 4—vii. 28
is written in Aramaic; a fact which may be accounted
for by supposing that the original Hebrew of this was
lost through the mutilation of a MS, and that the
deficiency was made good (previous to the translation of
the book into Greek) from an Aramaic Targum.

We can only conjecture what may have been the circumstances which conduced to the selection
(ii.) Circum-
stances of   of these books, and to their elevation to the
admission.   rank of Holy Scripture. But it is natural
to suppose that some striking historical events would have
produced a stronger appreciation of them than had
previously been felt; and that this would have raised

them, in due course, to their new position. A series of
events of the desired character may be found in the
circumstances which led to the Maccabaean revolt. And
when we read of how Antiochus Epiphanes tried to end
the Jewish nation and the Jewish religion at a single
blow ; and of how, with great subtlety, he attempted to
undermine the people's faith by the wanton destruction
of their sacred literature and other religious books ; we
can readily understand that, with the recovery of liberty
and the reconstruction of their social and religious life
under the Roman overlordship, the Jews would have
been inclined to attach a new value to works which had
come so near to perishing altogether. Thus, while it is
impossible to say definitely at what times and in what
order the various books were included, we may very
reasonably date the beginning of the process about the
year 160 B.C. While some of the books in question
would have obtained an easy and natural admittance to
the Canon, there is evidence pointing to the fact that
others were only granted their position after long consideration and with much hesitation. Such was the
case with the Song of Songs, Esther, Ecclesiastes and
Chronicles.

The long-standing feuds between the various re-
(iii.) Closing   ligious parties, and in particular between
of the Canon.   the Pharisees and the Sadducees, had their
origin in the political unrest generated during the
Hasmonaean period ; and it is exceedingly unlikely that
either party would ever have agreed to the addition of
any further books to the Canon at the instance of the
other. It is this consideration which leads us to date
the close of the process, by which the Kethubhim came
to rank as Scripture, about the year 100 B.C. Here,

then, we have the third great step in the formation of the
Old Testament Canon; and it was the last.

34. From this time forward the idea of a body of
Sacred Scripture attained an ever-increasing
rigidity. The possibility of additions was
excluded, and the text of the various books was gradually
reduced to conformity with a single standard or type.
By the times of our Lord the Hebrew Bible was practically what we possess to-day; and when, after the
destruction of Jerusalem in the year 70 A.D., the Jewish
leaders met in council at Jamnia (circ. 90–100 A.D.), the
inclusion of all our present books was ratified, and the
Canonicity and Sanctity of the Old Testament Scriptures
became, once for all, definitely and finally fixed and
recognised.

Synod of Jamnia.

35. It remains to say a few words about that large
class of Jewish literature which has come
down to us, some of which is included in
our Apocrypha, but none of which was
regarded as canonical. The division between those
books which, through their inclusion in the Apocrypha,
obtained a sort of quasi-canonicity in the early Christian
Church, and the rest, is really misleading. It is true
that our apocryphal books were included in the LXX,
and that they are there found distributed amongst the
canonical books, and not relegated to an appendix.
Moreover, though our MSS of the LXX are all from
Christian hands, it is certain that the copyists were
following, in this, the arrangement of the Greek-speaking
Jews of Alexandria. But there is no evidence to prove
that the books in question were ever regarded by the
Alexandrine Jews as canonical. We have already
observed that the LXX was never accorded the same

Apocrypha and Pseud-epigrapha.

reverence as was given to the Hebrew originals, and that no sense of propriety appears to have been shocked, in the first instance, by a loose rendering of the Hebrew, or by the addition, in some places, of copious editorial matter. Thus, when other books were circulated with the copies of the canonical writings, nothing would have been implied as to their status in relation to the Scriptures proper. In the same way, it would have been largely a matter of accident, or of individual choice, as to what books in particular should have been so circulated; and the selection did not mark them off as belonging to a class apart from the wider literature which is essentially of the same character. The word 'apocrypha' signifies 'hidden'; and it is possible that some, though obviously not all, of these works were regarded as being of an esoteric character, and designed for the study of the elect few, rather than for the mass of the people. In Alexandria the Hellenistic Jews came in contact with Greek philosophy; and, under that influence, they developed a theory that, for the few cultured initiates, there was a secret wisdom to be had, handed down from early times by tradition, and wrapped up in allegorical form in the Scriptures themselves. This theory had its affinities with the Hellenic mysteries and heathen magical ideas; and it appeared both in the Christian Gnostic heresies, and in the later Jewish Kabbalah. And it is reasonable to suppose that some of the early Wisdom literature and apocalyptic writings would have constituted a class which, in the opinion of Jewish scholars, was not suited to the ordinary reader. Hence their name 'Apocrypha.' But used as we use it, the name is not really applicable to the whole of the books it is chosen to include.

The word 'pseudepigrapha' merely describes the fact that the books, to which it is applied, were issued under the name of some other person than the author, who preferred to remain anonymous. But just as the term 'apocrypha' belongs of right to many books which were not included in the LXX, so that of 'pseudepigrapha' applies to several which were so included. Thus we may treat this whole literature as one; and, to repeat what we have said before, there is no precise reason, on the score of Inspiration, why the greater part of it should not have been included in the Canon of Scripture. That it was not so included is probably due to two circumstances of an accidental nature; the first being that the majority of these books, at any rate in their present form, were of too late a date to command general assent; and the second, that they were, many of them, originally written in Greek. To the character of the apocalyptic literature as a whole, its influence upon and use by the early Christian Church, and to the fact that much of it has been edited by Christian hands, we shall recur later on.

We must now, as briefly as possible, pass these books in review, roughly classifying them according to the nature of their contents, and suggesting for each of them a date, in some cases fairly certain, in others only probable. To commence with the historical writings; the book known as 1 Esdras appears to be a rendering from the Hebrew of Ezra, independent of the LXX translation, made perhaps about the year 140 B.C.; and it includes an original Greek composition (iii. 1—v. 6), an adaptation of a Persian story perhaps, which bears some resemblance to the Letter of Aristeas, and may have been composed at

Their dates and authorship.

about the same time; i.e. circ. 150 B.C.   2 Maccabees, which covers the period 175–160 B.C., was written in Greek and based upon a lost work by one Jason of Cyrene; its date may be about 120 B.C.   It is not nearly so reliable as 1 Maccabees, which covers the period 175–135 B.C.; a book of first-rate importance and of a high order of historical writing, composed by a Palestinian Jew in Hebrew, probably about the year 90 B.C.   Under the heading of apocalyptic writings we may group the following eight books.   The most important is the book of Enoch; a compilation from several sources, partly Hebrew and partly Aramaic, but now only found in translations, which may be dated, respectively, between the years 175 and 64 B.C.   The Testaments of the Twelve Patriarchs, originally written in Hebrew, was the work of a Pharisee, and may be dated exactly in 109–107 B.C. The Psalms of Solomon, also of Pharisaic origin, but of a somewhat different complexion, may be given to the period 63–48 B.C.   In the Secrets of Enoch we have a later work, which probably originated in Alexandria somewhere in the first half of the first century of the Christian era.   The Assumption of Moses is also a Pharisaic work, first written in Hebrew, which belongs to the period 7–30 A.D.; and the Apocalypse of Baruch, which exists in a Syriac translation of the Hebrew, seems to have been composed after the fall of Jerusalem in 70 A.D.   The Ascension of Isaiah is a composite work, and falls into three divisions, two of which are Christian and one, originally known as the Martyrdom of Isaiah, and which belongs to the latter part of the first century A.D., Jewish.   The last of these books, 2 Esdras, is also a compilation.   The main body of it, chapters iii—xiv, consists of three or more Apocalypses, written respectively between the years 70 and 100 A.D.; and to this chapters i and ii, xv and xvi were added at a very much later date—probably about 270 A.D. Two books fall under the heading of Wisdom, or proverbial, literature; Ecclesiasticus, which was written about 180 B.C. by Jesus ben Sirach in Hebrew and translated into Greek by his grandson in 130 B.C. (a portion of the original Hebrew, xxxix. 15—xlix. 11, has recently been discovered); and Wisdom, the production of a Greek-speaking Jew of Alexandria, somewhere in the first century before Christ. Several books there are which we may, perhaps, for convenience classify under the heading of Fable. The book of Tobit, a Greek work to be dated about 150 B.C.; Judith, originally in Hebrew, about 100 B.C.; some Greek additions to the canonical book of Esther, which may also belong to somewhere about the year 100 B.C.; sundry Greek additions to the canonical book of Daniel, which may fall a little later,—the Prayer of Azaria, the Song of the Three Children, Bel and the Dragon, and the History of Susanna; 3 Maccabees, which is a Greek production of a Jew of Alexandria, also in the first century B.C.; and 4 Maccabees, which probably falls as late as the year 30 A.D. The remaining books, which do not exactly come under any of the above headings, are the following. The book of Jubilees, a Pharisaic midrash, or allegorical commentary on portions of Scripture, originally written in Hebrew, may be dated somewhere in the period 140–110 B.C. The book of Baruch is a compilation; the first part, i—iii. 8, of which the original was in Hebrew, belongs to about the year 150 B.C.; the second part, composed in Greek (iii. 9—v), to somewhere a little after 70 A.D.; and the third part, the Epistle of Jeremiah (vi), also to the first century of the Christian era. The Prayer of Manasses may probably be given to the first century before Christ. The Sibylline Oracles is in the main a Christian work; but the third book is in part the composition of a Jew of Alexandria, and may be dated perhaps as early as 160 B.C. The Odes of Solomon, recently discovered in a Syriac dress, may have a Jewish foundation, though they have been worked up by Christian hands; and a Zadokite work, also quite recently discovered, exists in Hebrew in a fragmentary condition. But the dates of both these last books are still very uncertain. Such, in brief, are the various members of this extra-canonical Jewish literature.

36. One further remark needs to be made. We The Old Testa- have noticed that, before a definite type of ment, in its text was set up, a large number of MSS final form, inspired. were in existence, giving many various readings. These were set aside by a process of exclusion which was not, from our critical point of view, sound. Further, we have observed that the majority of the books were formed by a process of compilation and editing, which must leave us very dubious as to what were the actual words of the original, inspired, authors. The analysis of the books into their sources is very important from an historical and religious point of view; but the results of this work must frequently remain vague and uncertain. In that case it may be asked, 'What becomes of the theory of Inspiration? Are we to accept as inspired only what we can trace back to the original authors?' The answer, clearly, must be in the negative. For if the original narrative or prophecy was inspired, we are compelled to allow that the religious genius which appreciated, selected, edited and preserved it, was no less inspired. The Hebrew Bible, as it reaches us in its final form, is God's inspired Word for us.

BIBLIOGRAPHY.

WEIR: 'History of the Hebrew Text of the Old Testament.' (Williams and Norgate. 1907.)

GEDEN: 'Introduction to the Hebrew Bible.' (T. and T. Clark. 1909.)

DRIVER: 'Notes on the Hebrew Text of the Books of Samuel'; Introduction, pp. i—lv. (Clarendon Press. 2nd ed. 1913.)

RYLE: 'The Canon of the Old Testament.' (Macmillan. 2nd ed. 1904.)

SWETE: 'An Introduction to the Old Testament in Greek.' (Cambridge University Press. 1902.)

RAGG: 'The Book of Books'; chaps. 2, 3 and 4. (Arnold. 1910.)

BENNETT: 'A Biblical Introduction'; Part I, Old Testament. (Methuen. 1911.)

DRIVER: 'An Introduction to the Literature of the Old Testament.' (T. and T. Clark. 8th ed. 1910.)

ROBERTSON SMITH: 'The Old Testament in the Jewish Church.' (Black. 2nd ed. 1895.)

DAVIDSON: 'The Theology of the Old Testament.' (T. and T. Clark. 1904.)

CHARLES: 'The Apocrypha and Pseudepigrapha of the Old Testament, in English.' 2 vols. (Clarendon Press. 1913.)

HASTINGS: 'Dictionary of the Bible.'

CHEYNE AND BLACK: 'Encyclopædia Biblica.'
The relevant articles on the Text, Canon, Legal, Historical and Prophetical Literatures.

CHAPTER III

THE TEXT, CANON AND LITERATURE OF THE
NEW TESTAMENT

1. It will be convenient, in dealing with the New
Testament, to preserve the distinctions we

Difference
between
Criticism of
N.T. and that
of O.T.

adopted in the last chapter, and to speak
successively of the Text, the Canon, and
of those various problems which may be
grouped together as falling within the province of
Literary Criticism. But before we proceed further, one
remark of a general character may be made here, with a
view to relieving a certain apprehension to which the
last chapter may have given rise. The Old Testament
was originally the Bible of the Jewish Church. To the
earliest Christian communities it had all the sanctity and
authority of Scripture, and was still the sole Library of
Divine Revelation. The Christian writings at the first
took their place side by side with the Hebrew; and, so
far from ousting them from their pre-eminence, they were
rather received under the shelter and protection of the
Jewish Scriptures, as the conception of inspiration was
extended to cover and include them. But in course of
time it could not fail that, for Christian readers, a
peculiar significance came to be attached to the Christian
documents; so that, while the Old Testament was still
read as prophetic of Jesus Christ, the New Testament

came to have a value to which the Jewish writings could
not lay claim. Thus it is felt, and very reasonably felt,
that it is of greater and more fundamental importance
that the Christian records should be above suspicion, for
their accuracy and reliability, than those of the Old
Testament; and much of the disquiet to which the
criticism of the Old Testament has given rise is undoubtedly due to a fear lest the same processes should
overthrow our confidence in the New Testament. It is,
therefore, worth our while to notice, at the outset, that,
in passing from the Hebrew to the Christian Scriptures,
we leave behind us in large measure that element of
uncertainty as to the original and authentic utterances
of inspired men, the historical character of recorded
events, and so forth, which constantly meets us in our
study of the Old Testament, and which learned investigation can never hope entirely to remove. The reasons
for this higher confidence in the New Testament writings
are many, and they will be elaborated in due course; but
we may mention, at this point, two in particular. The
first, which applies to the Gospels and Acts, is that the
records they contain are very nearly contemporary with
the events, and are not divided from them by the space
of some hundreds of years, as was the case in the Old
Testament. And the second is that the MSS in our
possession, unlike those of the Old Testament, are not
only very many, but are some of them very ancient, and
are therefore removed from the actual autographs by
a relatively short interval of time. In other words, there
has been far less opportunity for the corruption of the
text. It is of course true that uncertainties of a kind do
exist, and that these are, in some cases, grave. We shall
have our attention drawn to them at a later stage. But

it may be said, with some emphasis, that the same sort
of insecurity which confronts us in our study of the Old
Testament has no justification whatever in the field of
New Testament criticism.

    2.   With this introductory remark, we may now turn
The Greek of   to consider the textual criticism of the
the N.T.   inspired Christian writings ; and, as was the
case with the Old Testament, we must preface what has
to be said with some account of the language in which
the early Christian authors expressed themselves. This
language was Greek ; a fact which need cause us no
(*a*) Univer-   surprise when we reflect upon the very wide
sality of Greek   range of the use of Greek in the then known
language.   world. Greek was indeed very largely spoken
in Rome itself, the world's centre, by all classes of the
populace, educated and uneducated alike. It was the
language of commerce throughout the Mediterranean,
being spoken by merchants, traders and sailors. It was
the one tongue which would carry a traveller almost
anywhere, enabling him to hold intercourse with the
inhabitants of most countries foreign to him. Jews of
the dispersions, that is to say Jews who, for various
reasons were living in colonies far from their own land,
forgot their native Aramaic and acquired the language
of the country of their adoption ; but, in addition to this,
they invariably possessed themselves of Greek, which,
amongst other purposes, enabled them to hold communication with each other ; and thus, in the New Testament,
these foreign Jews are always known as Hellenists, or
Greek-speaking, to distinguish them from the native
Hebrews, or Aramaic-speaking, Jews. But even so, the
difference of language presented no obstacle to intercourse between the home-staying Jews and those who

lived in exile from their native land. Jerusalem and
Judaea were, indeed, comparatively free from the influences of foreign culture and alien customs; but not so
Galilee and the sea-coast, which, under the Herodian
rule, had become very deeply infected with the ideas,
and had to a considerable extent adopted the language,
of the outside world. Thus a very large proportion of
home-staying Jews were probably bi-lingual; and even
amongst the peasant population there were many who
were as familiar with Greek as with their own Aramaic.

(b) Its adop-
tion by early
Church.
It is most likely that, in the earliest days,
Christians living in and around Jerusalem
may have committed to writing utterances,
and incidents in the life, of our Lord, couched in Aramaic;
indeed we have evidence for the existence of one such
document, though all are now lost to us. But so soon as
the outbreak of persecution began to drive the Christian
community further afield, and the conception of a mission,
first to the Jewish dispersions and then to the whole
Gentile world, presented itself to the mind of the infant
Church, then of necessity Greek became the medium of
communication between Christians all over the world,
and Christian evangelists, historians, letter-writers and
seers, expressed themselves in the only tongue which
would have been universally intelligible.

Until very recently the Greek of the old world was
(c) Distinction
between Greek
of N.T. and
that of
classical
writers.
known to scholars only in and through the
pages of the great authors of classical
antiquity; historians, philosophers, poets
and so forth. The Greek that flowed from
their pens naturally formed a standard of cultured diction;
and the student who would acquire Greek was instructed
to express himself in like fashion. And the result of

this has been that the scholar has been led to regard the writings of the New Testament with a certain degree of prejudice; for, by comparison with his favourite authors, he has found them to be lacking in the niceties of phrase and idiom which his studies have endeared to him; and, as a result, he has discovered them to be full of wanton obscurities which grammars and dictionaries failed to clear up. Consequently he has been disposed to dismiss them as examples of bad Greek. This prejudice is no new thing. In the early Christian centuries it was thought desirable to wean Christians from the study of heathen authors, whose pages were often marred by immoral and irreligious ideas; and more than one Church Father felt acutely the difficulty of substituting the Scriptures amongst the more cultured classes, whose literary taste was offended by their want of style. More

(*d*) Theory of a special Biblical Greek.

recently Christian scholars have attempted to account for this marked difference in the manner of writing; and a theory was manufactured which, in effect, said that the inspired writings demanded a diction of their own, and are written in what was called Biblical Greek. In proof of this was urged a great similarity with the Greek translation of the Old Testament, the Septuagint, and the frequency of 'Hebraisms'; by which was indicated the cases in which the idiom of the Hebrew language appeared to be literally transferred to the Greek. But within the last

(*e*) New linguistic evidence;

few years this theory has been entirely overthrown by the study of a great tract of ancient material which scholars had previously neglected. From all parts of the ancient world inscriptions on stone and metal have been collected; and from old rubbish heaps in Egypt and elsewhere the spade has unearthed a vast mass of fragmentary writings, on papyrus, wood, pot-sherds and what-not, dealing with every imaginary circumstance of daily life, from a magical charm or an official rescript to a school-boy's letter or a tradesman's bill. A study of these documents has revealed to us the fact that, up to the present, we have been accustomed to gauge the character of ancient Greek entirely from the products of literary art; an art which, in the later centuries, was far further divorced from the speech of everyday life than is the case with our modern authors. Now we have presented to us, for the first time, the vernacular; and the discovery has thrown great light upon the writings of the New Testament. It is now recognised that, with a few exceptions, of which the Epistle to the Hebrews is the most conspicuous, these writings were in the first instance casual productions which made no claim to any literary merit; that their authors had, in other words, no idea of making a book for the use and instruction of posterity, and that they therefore employed the ordinary spoken tongue which was in use all around them. This 'common' Greek was, as we have seen, in use all over the empire, from Alexandria to Ephesus and Athens, and from Galilee to Rome. It is probable that it possessed, in different quarters, dialectical peculiarities due to the influence of the native languages with which it came in contact; but on the whole it appears to have been remarkably similar all the world over. And this is the language of the New Testament; and a knowledge of it goes far to dissolve many of the obscurities which formerly troubled the expositor, and to make the interpretation of our authors in some respects a matter of greater certainty.

(f) which gives us the Greek vernacular, the language of the N.T.

It is true that this does not account for all the peculiarities noticeable in the language of the Christian writers.
There are still Hebraisms to be found, and a large inter-
mixture of the language of the LXX; but the latter
may probably be held to account for the former.   The
early Christians knew and studied their Old Testament
in the Greek version; and where they did not consciously
imitate its style, they often unconsciously reproduced the
phrases with which they were familiar.   And the LXX,
which represents several different levels of a translator's
capacity, frequently renders with some literalness the
idiom of the Hebrew original.   But in the main it may
be affirmed that the language of the New Testament is
just the Greek of common parlance throughout the
empire, which recent discovery and investigation have
resuscitated for us.

3.   Leaving then the question of the language of the
Textual
criticism.
Christian Scriptures, we come to that of the
text.   Here again, as was the case with
the Old Testament, the textual critic has to determine
what it was that the authors actually wrote.   And to
make the nature of his task clear, it will be necessary to
exhibit something of the materials with which he has
to deal; and, in doing so, it will become apparent that
the textual criticism of the New Testament differs in
some important features from that of the Old.

4.   The main difference may be stated as follows.
Difference
from textual
criticism of
the O.T.
The existing MSS of the Old Testament
are, as we have seen, all of one type; and
that type is the result of what we may call
a late revision conducted by uncritical editors.   If we
would go behind that in search of a more correct text,
we have, practically, only one direct piece of evidence to

help us, namely the Septuagint; for, with the exception of the Samaritan, and of the Aramaic Targums, so far as we know the Hebrew Scriptures were translated into no other language than Greek previous to the Christian era. Thus, the emendation of the Massoretic text must remain very largely a matter of rational conjecture. On the other hand, the existing MSS of the New Testament present us with three, if not four, distinct types of text; and the various readings they contain are exceedingly numerous. Moreover we possess, in several early translations, Latin, Syriac, Coptic and others, together with copious quotations in other Christian authors, a great mass of evidence which is of exceeding value. From all this material by far the greater part of the text of the originals can be reconstructed with absolute confidence and certainty; and in the comparatively few places where dubiety reigns it is almost unquestionable that the true reading is preserved in one or other of the existing variants. Thus in the textual criticism of the New Testament the exercise of conjecture is almost, if not entirely, excluded; and the task of the critic is to decide upon the respective values of his authorities, and to select his readings accordingly. But this necessarily implies a very intricate process of reasoning, of which we must proceed to give some account.

5. That period of intellectual culture which we have

The early printed editions of the N.T., and the ' Received Text.' learnt to call the Renaissance saw the revival of the study of Greek, which for centuries had been a dead language to all but a few obscure scholars. During all that period of ignorance, the Scriptures were known to the world at large only in a Latin translation; while important MSS of the original Greek lay neglected and forgotten in private and

monastic libraries. The Hebrew Old Testament, in its
entirety, had been in print for six and twenty years,
however, before the publication of the New Testament
in Greek was at length enterprised; and then the
honours were divided between two scholars of world-
wide reputation. The first edition to be printed was
that prepared under the direction of Cardinal Ximenes
in 1514; but as this was not published until six years
later, the edition by Erasmus in 1516 was the first in the
hands of the public. These, and other editions which
followed, were however eminently uncritical; that is to
say, their editors did not think of going behind the MSS
which lay ready to their hand, and, by comparing them
with those of far more ancient date, arriving at a text
more nearly approximating to the lost originals. Erasmus,
for instance, made use of five MSS only, which were at
his disposal at Basle; one of which belonged to the
11th century, and the others were all of later date. And
these MSS differed only in minor details, all of them
representing one type of text, which had been for
centuries reproduced by the professional copyists and
had been stereotyped by their labours. The first edition
of the Greek Testament to take notice of divergent
readings, and to adopt certain corrections into the text,
was that of Stephanus in 1546; and this was followed
by the Elzevir edition of 1624. The text so printed
was, until recent years, the standard and basis of all
New Testament study, and it was that from which our
own Authorised Version was translated; thus it was
usual to speak of it as the 'Received Text.'

6. When scholars came to turn their attention to
Beginnings of the old MSS, for more than two centuries
critical work. their work consisted mainly in the collection

of an enormous mass of material, by the careful reading and comparison of one document with another, which they left to posterity to utilise. And it was not until last century that scholars ventured to do more than annotate the Received Text with these alternative readings. But for more than fifty years the textual critics have been making the final advance. Putting aside the Received Text, they have set themselves the task of producing a new and independent text, based upon all the critical material which prolonged study has placed at their disposal ; and for this purpose they have attempted to determine the dates and localities of the various MSS, and their respective values and importance.

7. When we pass behind the late documents upon
The kinds of which our Received Text was based, we
material. find ourselves confronted by a continuous stream of evidence, an enormous mass of MSS, amounting to many thousands, which belong to every century from the 4th to the 15th ; fragments on papyrus, uncial codexes written on vellum, parchment cursives and even paper minuscules,—to employ terms which will presently be explained. It will simplify matters if we begin with the earliest productions, and work our way down through the centuries ; going on afterwards to speak of the translations and patristic quotations. But in the first place a few words are due to the external forms which, at different periods, the Scriptural writings assumed.

8. We have already noticed that, at the opening of
the Christian era, the Hebrew canonical
Papyrus Rolls. books, those copies at least which were intended for liturgical use in synagogue or temple, were written upon skins, which were fashioned in a long narrow strip and fastened at either end to a wooden

roller; so that a reader perusing such a book would unroll the MS with one hand while he rerolled what he had read with the other. The roll was the universal form of the book in those early days; and private copies of the Hebrew Scriptures would also have assumed this form. But in the case of these the material employed would far more frequently have been papyrus than skins, as being less cumbrous and less expensive. The pith of the papyrus reed was prepared in such a fashion as to make a strong and durable sort of paper; and at the beginning of the Christian era papyrus was probably the sole material for writing upon, in general use, in east and west alike; for Papyri, as these documents have come to be named, are found equally in the rubbish-heaps of Oxyrhynchus and the lava-sealed houses of Herculaneum. It is true that amongst the poorer classes 'ostraca' (i.e. broken pieces of pottery) were frequently used when papyrus was unavailable; and in the second and third centuries vellum was coming more and more into use, especially for documents which were not of a literary character. But it can hardly be doubted that the majority, if not the whole, of our New Testament books were originally written upon papyrus.

9. Papyrus paper was prepared in sheets, which measured anything from six to eighteen inches in height; and a roll was formed by attaching several of these sheets together. It is probable that rolls of different fixed lengths were sold in the markets; and it may be that the respective lengths of some at least of the New Testament writings were determined by the size of the rolls obtained. The writing was distributed in narrow columns, sometimes as many as four to a sheet, the

Manner and materials of writing.

columns being set to the height and not to the breadth of the sheet. In the earliest times the writing was continuous, without any separation of words, sentences or paragraphs, and being destitute of accentuation and punctuation. Two kinds of writing were in vogue; the literary and the non-literary hands. The non-literary was a cursive hand-writing, which employed a small script (minuscule) of characters which could easily be linked on to each other. This would, in all probability, have been the script employed by the original authors of our New Testament books. The literary hand was one in which each letter was a capital (majuscule) carefully and separately formed; and its script came to be known as 'uncial' (probably meaning 'inch-long'), owing to the scribes' habit of forming their characters of a very large size. The copying of a document at once gave it a sort of literary flavour and importance; thus all the early MSS of our books are written in uncials.

10. The copyist's pen was a reed shaped for the purpose; his ink was a compound in which soot formed the principal ingredient. The Jewish communities possessed their professional scribes; and the copying of the Scriptures was with them a sacred task. But in the heathen world copying was a trade similar to our printers'; and the class and character of the document to be copied had its regular price. It is doubtful whether the earliest Christian societies would have employed the services of the professional copyists; the necessity for preserving a secrecy about these writings, the fear of being denounced in times of persecution, or the lack of interest the heathen copyist would have displayed in such unliterary productions, all point in the same direction;—namely, that the more educated

Copyists.

amongst the Christians would have given themselves
to the multiplication of copies of their sacred books.
When the empire became Christian of course the circumstances would have been very different; but it is
probable that by that time there existed schools, such
as that at Caesarea, in which much of this work was
done; and these in turn would have been the parents
of the monastic establishments, similar to the Benedictines
of the West, which from the 6th century onwards were
entirely responsible for the task.

11. The New Testament Papyri cover a period of
The existing from three to four centuries. Owing to the
Papyri MSS. very meagre nature of the fragments which
have reached us, they have no particular value for textual
purposes. Of some twenty MSS in all, the longest contains only about eighty-four verses of the Epistle to the
Hebrews. But the oldest of them probably reaches back
to the early years of the 3rd century; and, in the complete
disappearance of all the autographs (and we can hardly
expect to discover at any time the originals of what
were essentially occasional writings, and therefore subject
to all the ravages of time and circumstance), it is at least
profoundly interesting to come upon transcriptions which,
in some cases, fall within less than two hundred years of
the inditing of the originals.

12. The dating of MSS, it may be explained, is
Method of based upon what is called palaeographical
dating MSS. (ancient writing) evidence; that is to say,
a study of old MSS has shown how in the course of
time one type of writing has succeeded another in
different localities; and, by a reverse process of reasoning,
a knowledge of these types enables a scholar to assign
a new MS with some confidence to the century of its

production. At a later period a MS is often found to bear its own date, or some notes or comments which materially assist us in fixing its nativity with precision.

13. With the 4th century we reach a new epoch

<small>The Vellum MSS.</small> in the history of our MSS. Papyrus was still in use, and continued to be so for some while; but for all large and important works vellum had come to take its place; and in due course it entirely superseded it. Doubtless it had been discovered that vellum was a more suitable substance to write upon; certainly it was more durable, and probably it was cheaper. The last reason would count for much in the 4th century when, with the conversion of Constantine, the empire became Christian, and the demand for the multiplication of copies of the Scriptures became excessive. Before this time another change of great importance had taken place; and this was the substitution of the book for the roll. The 'codex,' as

<small>(a) The Codex.</small> a book was then named, meant originally the trunk of a tree; and, then, a writing tablet made of wood and covered with wax; and, again, a collection or heap of these. Thus it came to be applied to a collection or heap of sheets of papyri, the rudimentary book; and then to a similar pile of vellum. The vellum was prepared in large sheets which were folded many times to make a quire of pages; and quire was placed upon quire to form a book. In course of time the book came to be enclosed in wooden boards for its protection, and the bound volume thus made its appearance. The

<small>(b) Collection of writings in one book.</small> importance of this development, for our purpose, lies in the fact that the codex rendered possible for the first time the collection of all the sacred books in one volume.

Hitherto the separate writings had occupied separate rolls; and the indigence of the early Christian communities must often have resulted in the possession, by several local churches, of only a few of the books, whether of the Old or the New Testament. With the appearance of the vellum codex however the demand could have been more easily supplied; for, unlike papyrus, vellum could be prepared anywhere, and was consequently cheaper. The Jewish synagogues had been accustomed to preserve their sacred rolls in wooden chests, when they were not in use; and doubtless the Christians followed their example in this with respect to their papyri. In this way writings of a similar character would have found their way into the same chest; and this may have determined the groupings of the books in the early codexes, which do not by any means invariably give us the whole of the New Testament. Thus the Four Gospels, the Pauline Epistles, the Catholic Epistles with Acts, and the Apocalypse, seem to have formed four natural groups; within which a great variety of order is discoverable. The vellum codex was originally arranged as the papyrus had been, with several narrow columns of writing to each page; but gradually this gave way to the more convenient practice of a single length of line. The writing was of the uncial script from the 4th to the 10th century; when the capital type gave way before the introduction of the cursive.

14. At the present moment there are in existence 168 uncial codexes; or rather, since discovery often brings fresh MSS to light, this is the number now known to scholars. Of these 123 are short and comparatively unimportant; many of them, indeed, being mere fragments of a single leaf.

Existing Un-
cial Codexes.

The remaining 45 are, in varying degrees, of moment to the textual critic; and these are usually referred to by the symbolic use of characters provided by the Latin and Greek alphabets. Some few of these codexes are, but for slight mutilations, complete texts, not of the New Testament alone but also of the LXX version of the Old Testament; while others only embrace one of the four groups of books referred to above. Some of them provide a Latin version of the writings side by side with the Greek text; others are palimpsests; that is to say MSS in which a scribe has nearly obliterated the original copy of the Scriptures in order to transcribe above it the work of another author,—a practice which was common when parchment was scarce and expensive. Some are very simply or carelessly executed; others are prepared with great sumptuousness, with silver or gold lettering upon purple-stained vellum. Roughly we may apportion these 45 MSS to their respective centuries as follows; to the 4th century two, to the 5th six, to the 6th ten, to the 7th one, to the 8th three, to the 9th twenty, and to the 10th three.

15. Six of these stand out as possessing a pre-eminent value and importance; and we may enumerate them here, while leaving to a later stage an explanation of that in which their importance consists. The oldest of all, and, as investigation has proved, the most valuable for textual purposes, is the Codex Vaticanus; so called because it reposes in the Vatican library at Rome. It belongs to the 4th century, and is generally known by the symbol B. Next to this in point of antiquity, for it too comes to us from the 4th century, is the Codex Sinaiticus, which

Six of highest importance.

(a) Vaticanus.

(b) Sinaiticus.

was dramatically recovered from a monastery in Sinai by a travelling scholar in the middle of last century. The symbol chosen for it is the first letter of the Hebrew alphabet, ℵ. By a curious coincidence this MS also stands next to B in point of importance for textual scholars. The Codex Alexandrinus, spoken of as A, is so named because it was long associated with Alexandria, from whence it was carried to Constantinople in the year 1621; and the Codex Ephraemi, or C, is a palimpsest which bears upon its face the text of certain treatises by a Syriac theologian, St Ephraem—whence its name. These two both date from the 5th century. B, as we have said, now reposes at Rome; ℵ has found a home for itself in the Imperial library at St Petersburg; A is now to be found in the British Museum; while the Bibliothèque Nationale at Paris is the possessor of C. These four MSS originally contained the whole Bible; that is to say they included the LXX version of the Old Testament. And since A and B have suffered but little mutilation, they are also the principal authorities for the text of the LXX. The two other MSS which we described as being of the highest value are, first the Codex Bezae, known as D, which was at one time in the possession of the Swiss reformer Beza; and, second, the Codex Claromontanus, or D₂, which also belonged to Beza, and is named after the monastery of Clermont where he found it. Both of these possess Latin versions in addition to the Greek text, and they supplement each other; for whereas D contains the Gospels, Acts and Catholic Epistles only, D₂ has the Pauline Epistles but is lacking in all else. D, which is in the possession

(c) Alexandrinus.

(d) Ephraemi.

(e) Bezae.

(f) Claromontanus.

of the Cambridge University Library, dates from the 5th century; while D_2, now to be found in the Bibliothèque Nationale at Paris, belongs to the 6th.

16. Towards the end of the first millennium of the
The Cursive
MSS. Christian era there occurred, not all at once but by gradual degrees, a further change which marks the opening of a third epoch in the history of our MSS. This was the substitution of the cursive for the uncial codex. From very early days, as we have noticed, there existed side by side with the alphabet of capitals, which was exclusively used for literary purposes, a smaller type of script which was in daily use for all the practical demands of ordinary life. Now, for the first time, this minuscule alphabet was rescued from its lowlier usage, and raised to the dignity of literary associations. Doubtless the reasons for this change lay in the constantly increasing demand for copies of the sacred books; for the uncial type of writing would have been tedious and slow, and the uncial codexes were undoubtedly bulky and cumbrous, besides being expensive. Thus the cursive innovation effected an economy of space and time in the production of the volumes, and cheapened the price of sale. Vellum, or parchment, continued to be used by the copyists as the material for their labours; for though paper was already being manufactured in Europe in the 12th century, it was found to be less adaptable for writing upon than vellum, and it did not come at all largely into use for literary purposes until the introduction of printing. Of these cursive MSS, produced between the 10th and the 16th centuries, more than two thousand are known and catalogued, and probably very many more are hidden in libraries, monasteries and private collections throughout

Europe. They are indicated by numerical symbols;
but as yet the whole mass of them has not been ex-
haustively examined. It was, as we have seen, from
certain well-known cursives that Erasmus and other
early editors of the printed editions derived their text
of the New Testament.

17. Beside the cursive MSS we must place the
The Lection- lectionaries, or collections of chosen portions
aries. of Scripture appointed by the Church for
liturgical use, of which more than fifteen hundred are
known; though these again have not as yet been
thoroughly studied. They include uncials as well as
cursives; but none of the uncial MSS are earlier than
the 9th century.

18. It is now time to retrace our steps, and to
Types of enquire whither this enormous mass of
Text. evidence for the Greek text of the New
Testament leads us. We have already indicated that
a considerable difference exists between the types of
text with which our MSS present us; and we must
now discover what this difference is, and what it implies.
The six great uncial codexes, to which we have referred,
derive their importance not alone from their antiquity,
nor yet from their substantial agreement over the major
part of the text of the New Testament; though these
points are obviously of very special significance. It is
rather their differences which make them of unique value
to us; for, by a happy coincidence, time has preserved
to us in these six the main lines of textual tradition
which appear all down the ages. In other words, already
in the 4th and 5th centuries the text had diverged from
its original form, and become more or less fixed in
several distinct types; and these MSS give us those

separate types in all their essential features. The force of this remark will become more clear as we go on.

19. We have already alluded, in speaking of the Old Testament, to the natural, and in some cases almost inevitable, errors of the copyists;

The errors and corrections of the Copyists.

and we must recollect that the chances of error, errors of hand and of eye, would have been materially increased by the lack of our modern facilities for such work. For when the transcription had to be made from, and into, a somewhat unmanageable and flimsy roll, and without the use of a large and convenient writing table, an additional strain was constantly placed upon the memory. But to these natural causes of error, in the case of the New Testament documents we are bound to add others which would have been excluded in the Hebrew Scriptures by the idea of sanctity already attaching to the text. In the early days of transmission of the Christian writings, the scribe was more concerned to convey the sense than the actual wording of what was written ; hence he did not scruple to make corrections, grammatical and otherwise, where he felt they were needed, and to clear up obscurities by conjectural alterations. Nor did he hesitate to add points of interest which had reached him through some independent line of tradition,—words and even incidents left unrecorded by his author. In the first instance such corrections and additions will often have been jotted down in the margin, while a later scribe took upon himself the insertion of such glosses in the body of the text ; but in many cases undoubtedly the alteration will have been effected silently from the first. When we remember that copies of these writings were, as early as the 2nd century, being diffused throughout the empire; and that those copies were giving rise to innumerable others, the labour of very different kinds of men in widely separated localities; we shall easily perceive how inevitable it was that different types of text would have arisen and been perpetuated in different quarters of the ancient world.

20. Now a careful study of the principal uncial

Groups or families of MSS, and their genealogy.

codexes reveals, as we might have expected, this important point to begin with; namely that these MSS tend to group themselves in different families, according to the manner in which certain of them agree in respect of readings which they do not share with the rest. That is to say, such a family is constituted by the fact that all the MSS belonging to it reproduce, in the main, the same errors, the same corrections or additions, and other peculiarities of style. Again, it is quickly noticed that these families each fall into a number of smaller groups, having the same principal features in common, but differing from each other in minor points of detail. The marked similarity thus established between the various MSS which go to form such a family, taken in connection with the differences which divide the separate units of the family, can only be accounted for in one way; and that is best expressed by the symbol of a genealogical tree, of which they are severally the members. That is to say, in the long process of transcription, all the individual members of that family must have been derived from one specific ancestor, a parent MS now lost to us. In certain cases where two distinct families have corresponding features which appear to link them together, it is possible to travel a step further, and, recognising a distant cousinship between the lost ancestor of each, to postulate an original parent for both families. And in this way, though the earliest evidence is probably lost to us beyond hope of recovery, we should be able to trace all existing MSS, notwithstanding their differences, in a natural sequence back to one original, the inspired autograph.

21. And yet the matter is not nearly so simple as it sounds when thus stated. For the question of genealogical relationship is frequently complicated, especially in the case of the later MSS, by the fact that the copyists have evidently had before them two or more divergent authorities; the readings of which they have combined in different degrees according to their own fancy, thus producing a novel and, as it is called, a 'mixed' type of text. In this way we find members of different families in agreement with each other, and in disagreement with their own groups, in a manner which is very perplexing. But, as we shall see, a mixed type of text dates back to very early times; and it is not difficult to realise for ourselves the copyist's mental attitude, when, confronted by two or more variants, each of them interesting, he did not desire to sacrifice any of them.

Mixture of readings of different MSS.

22. As the result of patient and laborious research, scholars have come to recognise, in the existing uncial codexes, four separate and distinct types of text, which can all of them, in more or less entirety, be recovered from these MSS. That being so, it has been found convenient to utilise, in speaking of them, the four initial characters of the Greek alphabet, denominating the four types respectively the a, β, γ, and δ-text. It seems probable that each of these was, during a certain period and over a certain area, acknowledged

Four main types.

as the standard and correct text; and they were all of
them in existence at an early date,—that is to say at
the least by the 4th century. Moreover they were the
types from which have sprung all the MSS known to us,
and which may, by successive steps, be ultimately traced
back to them. It is therefore a singular thing to find
that three out of the four types of text are represented,
and not only represented but represented in their most
perfect form, by the most ancient codexes in our possession, namely the six we have previously enumerated.
We must say a few words about each of these types of
text in turn.

The *a*-text, which is so distinguished because it is
virtually identical with the Received Text
(*a*) The *a*-text.   of the early printed editions, is given in
its purest form by A. A study of this type of text
reveals the fact that, though it appeared certainly as
early as the year 380 A.D., it is already a mixed text;
that is to say, it weaves together readings found in the
other principal texts, and therefore is later than they
are. This conclusion is supported by a very significant
fact; which is, that these mixed or 'conflate' readings,
as they are called, which are the distinguishing characteristic of the *a*-text, do not appear in the writings of
any of the Christian fathers before the 5th century. In
fact they are first quoted by St Chrysostom ; and from
his time onward the *a*-text seems to have become the
standard, and consequently has more evidence in its
favour than any other. Its relatively late appearance,
the mixture of its readings, and the rapid popularity it
achieved, all point to the fact that the *a*-text was the
result of a deliberate and authoritative revision. Moreover, the fact that it was first used in the east, and

thence spread westwards, as can be proved from the
types of authors who quote it; and the additional fact
that, as we shall see, it is closely related to the great
Syriac translation known as the Peshitto; both direct
us to Antioch in Syria, the sometime capital of the
eastern empire, as the locality of its production.   It is
probable that the church in that country, harassed and
perplexed by the wide differences of contemporary
MSS, of which many different types were in existence,
felt the desirability of issuing a single authoritative text
for use in public worship; and further, that the revisers
were guided in their labours rather by the necessity of
edification than by critical principles, and therefore set
themselves to combine the various readings so far as
possible, rather than lose anything which appeared to
them as of some value.

The β-text differs the most widely from that
which we have just been considering, and
it possesses far less MS evidence than the
other.   This was held to be prejudicial to its claims,
when it was thought that the readings most likely to be
correct were the ones which could show a majority of
MSS in their favour.   But the genealogical connection
between documents has enabled us to realise that a
majority may be all lineally related to a single original,
possessing an excellence not comparable to that of a
MS which has but few descendants.   And recent investigation has so rehabilitated the β-text, that the vast
majority of scholars are now agreed in regarding it as
the most faithful of all to the lost originals.   The reason
which has led critics to this decision may be briefly
stated thus.   If a certain type of text is found to differ
from all other types in a great number of places, where

(b) The β-text.

on grounds of probability it must be confessed that all the rest present us with readings which are certainly erroneous, and this type alone with readings which are as certainly right ; then this particular type may reasonably be trusted in a large number of other readings where mere probability cannot help us to a decision. Thus, since the β-text has been found to fulfil the necessary conditions, it has been conceded a position of authority above all other types. And that this confidence is not misplaced is proved by the evidence in favour of the β-text, forthcoming from the oldest translations and patristic quotations. This type is best represented by B, which is thus not only our most ancient codex, but also our most valuable. B is found to be supported more frequently by ℵ than by any other existing codex ; and it follows that B and ℵ are both of them descended from a common ancestor, which in point of time would have been very little removed from the original autographs. It is impossible to say with any confidence where B was produced; but the evidence, which includes the affinity to it of the Coptic versions, seems to point to some sort of connection with the great Biblical scholar and critic Origen, and would therefore indicate one of the two important fields of his literary activity, Alexandria or Caesarea. The text of B is, in the opinion of those competent to judge, not only relatively the nearest approximation to the autographs we possess, but actually a very faithful and close reproduction of them. It has therefore come to be known as the 'neutral' text; the standard, that is, from which, in the main, other texts must be regarded as variants. This is not to say, however, that the β-text which it gives is infallible. It seems probable that its authors, whose guiding principle was the conservation of a traditional text in all its purity, must have had the sundry readings of the δ-text before them; and it is more than likely that in some cases they may have wrongly rejected them. In one small class of instances it is clear that this is what actually happened; namely where the δ-text, which as a rule adds to the originals, omits words which the β-text includes. These omissions by the δ-text, known by the rather formidable formula of 'Western non-interpolations,' ought, it seems, to have been accepted by the β-text. From this it follows that the work of the critic, though greatly simplified by the discovery of the unique value of B, is far from being ended.

Of the γ-text we have less to say, for the reason that it does not exist at the present day, as a continuous text, in any one MS. And yet it is more than a mere matter of conjecture that such a text did, at one time, have an independent existence; for not a little evidence for its readings may be found in MSS which blend them with another type of text. Its character seems to have been that of a scholarly revision, concerned amongst other things with the removal of grammatical faults and obscurities; and, as the evidence appears to connect it with Egypt, it is probable that it was the work of scholars associated with the university of Alexandria—whence it is now commonly known as the Alexandrian text. If this is so, then we may perhaps conjecture that the γ-text is related to the β-text, as a scholarly but uncritical revision is related to a carefully preserved tradition.

(c) The γ-text.

Last of all we reach the δ-text; in some respects the most interesting of all. Differing very widely from the β-text, in the majority of

(d) The δ-text.

cases it clearly does not contain the genuine reading. But it stands on a different footing from the a-text in that it is far more ancient.   Indeed, with the β-text, it is one of the two principal sources for the conflate readings of the a-text.   It is most fully represented by D and D_2, which as we have seen supplement each other.   It has generally been designated the 'Western' text, owing to a mistaken idea that it originated in Rome, or elsewhere in Italy.   This has been proved incorrect by the fact that several old versions, which reproduce this text, together with patristic writings which quote it, give it a far larger provenance than had been anticipated.   Thus the Old Latin version locates it in and about Carthage, the Old Syriac and Armenian versions give it to the East, and the quotations of Origen and Clement of Alexandria take it to Egypt.   It is now pretty generally recognised that the δ-text is not a fixed type such as are the others, but rather a symbol for a great diversity of various readings.   This may be explained as follows. In the earliest days of the transmission of the New Testament writings, the text was far more freely handled by the copyists than was the case at a later date, when their canonisation as Sacred Scripture guarded them from corruptions, in the same way in which the Hebrew Bible was protected. When we pass on to speak of the growth of the Canon, we shall see how slowly the conception of authority and inspiration arose to give its fostering care to the text of the Christian writings ; and how long a space of time elapsed for the introduction of corruptions and corrections and additions.   When copies of these writings were produced by the unprofessional hands of religious men, copies not for the adornment of a library but for diligent use in private circles and amongst poor

congregations; and when the MSS were in constant
danger of destruction during times of persecution, and
when no scholar's trained intelligence was available for
superintending the work; then, doubtless, what was
written was but roughly executed on cheap papyrus,
and such copies would have formed but poor and
unreliable exemplars for future scribes. And when the
momentary anticipation of the end of this present age
taught men to care far more for the religious substance
of these books, than for verbal accuracy in transcribing
them, it was but natural that they should both vary the
language where they felt disposed, and introduce into
their texts incidents and sayings which had reached
them from other quarters. It is this early and chaotic
period in the history of the text, when each preacher
of Christianity was an editor of the sacred books, which
is represented by the δ-text. Thus the δ-text, though
it may frequently preserve a genuine reading which
every other MS has lost, is truly the measure of the
inevitable mishandling of the originals by different
persons in different localities, and from different causes
and motives.

Thus, to sum up in a few words, the relations of
these four types of text to each other were
something of this sort. During the early
diffusion of the various books throughout
the world there was an initial period of corruption; and
this is brought before us principally in the great majority
of the variants of the δ-text. At the same time, owing
to the watchfulness and critical instinct of scholars such
as Origen, there was preserved in Egypt a far more
faithful type, the β-text; side by side with a definite
revision, the γ-text, which failed to obtain any wide

(e) Mutual relations of these types of text.

currency for itself. And then, in the 3rd and 4th centuries, a definite editing was undertaken at Antioch which resulted in the production of the *a*-text; and this text, owing to the authority which promulgated it, possibly, and protected by the newly-discovered principle of canonicity, gradually won its way to universal acceptance, ousting the other types, until it became stereotyped as the standard text of Christendom.

23. The cursive MSS and the lectionaries exhibit the same tendency as do the uncial codexes to fall into groups or families, connected with each other, and with the uncials, as members of a genealogical tree. As a rule, following our expectations, they exhibit a mixed type of text, and the majority fall on the side of the *a*-text. Nevertheless it is possible to dissever the strands of the other main types of text in them; and it is of course conceivable that a late MS may embody genuine readings, derived from a line of MSS now lost to us, which received little or no early support. But, in the main, we are not justified in looking for much independence in the cursives or lectionaries; and, relatively, they have no high degree of authority for the textual critic.

24. The case is otherwise with the early versions, or translations into other languages of the whole, or part, of the New Testament books; and to these we must now turn. The text of a version is based on the evidence of MSS, which have to be sifted and examined in the same fashion as those of the Greek text itself. In the case of some of the versions the text has been well and carefully preserved ; in the case of others it remains very frequently dubious. When the original text of a version has been restored, we are then in a position to argue back to the Greek idiom from which it was translated. Now the value of a version depends, to a great extent, upon the date at which the translation was made; and that is a point which has to be determined. If, as is the case with certain of them, a version may be cast back to a period antecedent to the oldest Greek MSS we possess, then it is obvious that the evidence it affords us for the text is of the most considerable value. It may not only support in general a particular type of text, but it may help us to recover a lost reading, or prove a reading genuine which has hitherto had but slight evidence in its favour. We may single out here the principal ancient versions which the textual critic is bound to take into account, giving a brief description of each.

There is, first of all, the Syriac. In the last chapter

(a) Syriac Versions.
(i.) Syriac Language.

we drew attention to the fact that the Aramaic speech, which is akin to the ancient Hebrew, was the vernacular in Palestine at the beginning of the Christian era, and was the language which Jesus and His disciples were in the habit of using in their daily intercourse. Since a large proportion of the members of the early Church were Palestinian Jews, and natives of Syria, it was natural that the New Testament documents should have been very soon translated into Aramaic, or Syriac as it was called in the northern provinces, for the benefit of those who knew no Greek. Judaea and Galilee each had their separate dialects of Aramaic; and the Syriac of the version is not quite the same as either, and is probably the dialect spoken in and about Antioch. We know that a harmony of the four Gospels, called the Diatessaron, was composed in Syriac by Tatian about the year 170 A.D.; but this work only exists in two translations at the present day, Arabic and Armenian. We have, however, two distinct types of text in two separate Syriac versions; one known as the Old Syriac, the other as the Peshitto.

The Peshitto, which means 'simple' (the precise implication of this designation is not clear), is the standard Syriac text, corresponding to the Latin Vulgate and our own Authorised Version; and until recent years it was the only Syriac text known. Some of the MSS in which it is found are very ancient, going back to the 5th century; and it is exceedingly probable that the version is identical with one known to have been made early in that century by one Rabbula, Bishop of Edessa. An examination of its text, which can be restored with great accuracy, and which contains the whole of the Old Testament besides the greater part of the New, proves it to have been a translation of the Greek *a*-text. But of late there has come to light, in two portions, another and more ancient Syriac version, which for textual purposes is of greater importance. This version contains the four Gospels only; and it has been reconstructed from what are known as the Curetonian MSS (which take their name from their first editor, Dr Cureton), and the Sinaitic, a MS discovered in a monastery on Sinai at the close of last century. It seems probable that these two, which supplement each other, are both derived from a common ancestor; and that this ancestor may be placed in the 2nd century, perhaps as early as Tatian's Diatessaron. As we should expect, this version exhibits the characteristics of the δ-text.

(ii.) The Peshitto.

(iii.) The Old Syriac.

Another version of first-rate importance is the Coptic.

(*b*) Coptic Versions. (i.) Coptic Language. The Coptic language was a survival of the ancient Egyptian; and it appears to have existed, during the early days of Christianity, in several distinct dialects, of which the principal were the Bohairic, spoken in Lower Egypt in the delta of the Nile, and the Sahidic, which obtained in Upper Egypt. With the exception of six characters, which stand for vocal sounds unknown to the Greek, the Coptic script is just the Greek alphabet; and it seems probable that the increasing Hellenic civilisation of Lower Egypt led to the disuse of the more cumbrous demotic and hieroglyphic signs. Like the Syriac, the Coptic has two separate versions, one in each of the two principal dialects, besides some very fragmentary remains of versions in other dialects, about which very little is at present known. The existing Coptic MSS are in one particular very dissimilar to the Greek, in that they present us with very few, and those but trifling, various readings. And this extreme care and accuracy of the Coptic copyists has put into our hands a singularly pure text of the original translations; with the result that we are in a position to estimate with considerable confidence the character of the Greek text from which the transla-

(ii.) The Bohairic. tions were made. The Bohairic version has the greater literary merit, as would be expected from the locality of its birth; and, owing to this superior excellence, it seems to have gradually super-

(iii.) The Sahidic. seded the Sahidic version in its general use. On the other hand the Sahidic version is probably by some fifty years or so the elder of the two, and may date from the early years of the 3rd century. It is noteworthy that all the most ancient Coptic MSS, of which one on papyrus may come from the 4th century, testify to the Sahidic version; but this is probably due to the accident that the extreme dryness of the climate of Upper Egypt has preserved to us documents which could scarcely have survived in Lower Egypt. The Coptic versions are of great value to the textual critic because they reproduce, in the main, the β-text, though with a leaven of readings characteristic of the δ-text.

The third of the ancient versions which rank amongst the most important is the Latin. As is the case with the Syriac, so in the Latin there exists a translation which for centuries has held the field as the standard version of the Scriptures in the Western world, having been used alike for liturgical purposes and for private study, namely the Vulgate; and, side by side with this, what is known as the Old Latin version, a more ancient translation which has only recently yielded up its fruits to enquiring scholarship, and which proves to be, from the textual point of view, far the more interesting of the two.

(c) Latin Versions.

It was at one time erroneously supposed that Christianity in Rome would have demanded for itself, at a very early date, a Latin translation of the New Testament writings. It is now recognised (and we have already called attention to the fact) that the capital of the world was, at that date, Hellenised to a very considerable degree, and that Greek undoubtedly was the language of the primitive Roman Church. We know as a matter of fact that a Greek liturgy served its purposes at least until near the close of the 2nd century. Thus we are not surprised to discover that the earliest Latin version of the New

(i) Old Latin.

Testament had its origin in northern Africa, where Latin was almost universally spoken; in and about Carthage, where Christianity fixed its roots at a very early date. The great African fathers, Tertullian and Cyprian, undoubtedly quote Scripture from a Latin translation; and this fact would seem to cast back such a version well towards the middle of the 2nd century. But in speaking of the version which has actually reached us, we are met by the difficulty that the existing MSS, which though mostly very fragmentary are often of an early date, differ profoundly amongst themselves. From this we are led to infer that we are, in reality, dealing with more than one Old Latin version; and we may conjecture that, if some of the MSS represent an original African translation, others give us portions of other and later translations enterprised at various dates in Italy and elsewhere. And this theory of a multiplicity of versions is supported by the conditions which, as we know, led to the great 4th century revision which goes by the name of the Vulgate. The original African translation seems to have presented a variety of the

(ii.) The 𝛿-text. Of the Vulgate, the Bible of the
Vulgate. Roman Church, it is impossible to speak here otherwise than very briefly. Towards the end of the 4th century Pope Damasus requested St Jerome, the greatest living Biblical scholar of those days, to undertake a new and authoritative Latin translation of the whole Bible. The Old Testament he retranslated, not from the LXX, but from the original Hebrew. The New Testament, however, was not so thoroughly treated; for he contented himself here with publishing a revision of the Old Latin texts, by a comparison of their readings with those of the Greek MSS to which he had access.

B. 9

The Gospels, which he bestowed most care upon, appeared in the year 383 A.D., and the rest of the writings, which he dealt with in a more perfunctory fashion, at a later date. The Vulgate was, it will be observed, an official version of the Scriptures, undertaken and published by authority. For this reason it was bound to, and in course of time actually did, supersede the use of the Old Latin versions. But the history of the Vulgate has been similar in certain respects to that of the Greek text itself; which is to say that, for various reasons, it has suffered by corruption and correction; with the result that the MSS are often at variance with each other. In consequence of this the Vulgate, which was itself a revision, has often been revised. The number of codexes still at the disposal of the critic is enormous, exceeding indeed eight thousand; and of these several of the most important are also of great antiquity, and are referred by scholars to the 5th and 6th centuries. Soon after the invention of printing there appeared an edition of the Vulgate, the famous Mazarin Bible printed at Gutenberg in 1456; but, like the edition of the Greek Testament by Erasmus, this was in no sense a critical production. Stephanus was the first to lead off, in 1528, with an attempted reconstruction of the original text; and this pioneering work has been followed, up to our own day, by editions of greater accuracy. It appears, from the labours that have been bestowed upon the text, that in the revision of the Old Latin versions Jerome relied mainly upon the evidence of that type of text which to-day is represented by א; which is to say that the Vulgate is a witness to the diffusion in the West of the β-text, which we know as the neutral or standard type.

25. So much then for the versions. But one important body of evidence for the text of
the New Testament still remains for us to
glance at; and that is the evidence supplied
by quotations found in the writings of the Christian
fathers. In general it may be said that if a father, in
quoting a passage from the New Testament, follows a
particular form of words, that is evidence that the MS
he used contained that particular reading. And if that
reading is distinctive of a particular type of text, then
his MS was of that type. And further, if the author in
question lived and wrote in the 3rd or 2nd centuries,
then his quotations provide us with evidence for the text
older than that of any existing MS. But this general
proposition must be modified by a variety of considerations. In the first place the patristic writings themselves
depend for us on the evidence of MSS; and before we
can use them for textual purposes, with any confidence,
we must be sure that we have before us what the author
actually wrote. In the next place, we are bound to
make allowances for the fact that a writer will often
have depended upon his memory in quoting, without
verifying the words by reference to his roll or codex;
and the context of the quotation must be studied, to
discover the use to which it is put, before we can be
sure of what his authority gave him. And, again, in the
case of the Latin fathers, it often happens that they
translate freely from a Greek original rather than quote
from an existing Latin version. Moreover, in the copying
of the patristic writings many an interesting reading
will have been lost, owing to the tendency of the
copyists to assimilate the quotations to the type of
text most familiar to themselves. But when all these

considerations have been given their due weight, it will frequently happen that a quotation by a father gives support to a reading for which there is but slender evidence in the MSS; and, in addition, it may help to determine where, and at what time, such a reading came into existence. The bearing of patristic quotations upon the question of the text cannot very well be elucidated without copious illustration; but in general it may be affirmed that a tendency is observable from a use of the δ-text in the earlier, to that of the a-text in the later writers. Up to about the middle of the 2nd century, patristic quotations are few and indirect. In accordance with the liberty in the treatment of Scripture which, as we have seen, distinguished the early Church, when the sense rather than the actual words was considered of primary importance; and, further, owing to the scarcity of MSS, and the difficulties encountered in the hunting up of references inseparable from the use of MSS which contained no divisions of chapter and verse, both of which causes implied a large measure of trust in an often precarious memory; the usual habit of these earlier writers was, reference to Scripture either by free allusion or by conscious paraphrase. But, with the growth of the conception of canonicity, and from the times of Irenaeus onwards, there is observable an ever-increasing care, accuracy and explicitness in the matter of quotations.

26. It is now time that we should pass to the second of the three subjects of the present chapter, the history of the Canon of the New Testament. We may recall, in the first place, what we said in dealing with the Hebrew Scriptures about the meaning of canonicity. It implies,

History of the Canon of the N.T.

roughly, that there exists a certain body of writings to which the Church has set her seal that they are, in her opinion, divinely inspired and given as an authoritative standard and regulation of the moral and religious life within her communion.   Without denying the possible inspiration and usefulness as a means to edification of other writings, the Christian consciousness has, by a continuous judgment pronounced through successive ages, selected, accepted and guaranteed these writings, and these alone, for such a purpose.   By the opening of the 5th century the Canon of the New Testament appears to have been, for all practical purposes, closed ; and the result was what we possess at the present day.   But the problem before us is to discover by what process that result was achieved, and how a canonical body of inspired Christian documents was built up, so that it came to out-rival in sanctity the older volume of the Jewish Scriptures. As was the case with the Old Testament, we shall find that the successive stages in this history are shrouded in obscurity, owing to the fact that the Christian writings were in no case officially promulgated until they had already received the tacit sanction of the Church at large. Nevertheless a study of the circumstances in which they came to their own, reveals sufficiently clearly the principles and motives which underlay the process, and brings to light certain land-marks which will claim our attention.

27.   The evidence at our disposal for tracing the history of the New Testament Canon, is to be found in other early Christian productions, the writings of the Christian fathers and of those who are known to Church history as heretics, and in the formal decrees of councils.   We begin with allusions and

The kinds of evidence.

quotations, which prove that such and such a book was known and used by the writer and his readers ; we pass on to quotations which are of such a form as to exhibit the fact that this and that book was already coming to be regarded as authoritative, and regulative of the faith and morals of the Christian communities ; we reach lists of such books, drawn up independently by various fathers with the avowed intention of defining what were and what were not, in their opinion and practice, fitted for public reading and private study ; and finally we have the conciliar decisions, which indicate a final and universal approval of the writings which the judgment of preceding generations had thus selected. It is, of course, not possible to present this kind of evidence here ; and we must content ourselves with indicating the conclusions reached by scholars upon a study of all the material, and with sketching in outline the general course of events which led to the completion of the Canon.

28. In the early days of Christianity the Church Christian use was possessed of one Testament, or Canon of the LXX. of Scripture, only ; and that was the Jewish Bible. Since the almost universal language of the early Church was Greek, it was inevitable that the Jewish Scriptures should have been known almost exclusively in the LXX version ; and most of our New Testament writings bear witness to the use and influence of this version. But Christian theology started from a belief that Jesus was the Christ, the fulfilment of prophecy ; and in consequence of the conviction that the Old Testament was mainly concerned with the Person of their Master, the Christian communities naturally came to regard the Jewish Scriptures as being pre-eminently a

Christian Bible, the rightful possession of the Christian Church.   Indeed their appropriation of the LXX appears to have been so exclusive, that the unconverted Jews were driven to making another translation for their own use, that of Aquila.   Now the habit of the Christian writers in citing the Old Testament, a habit which indicates the great reverence in which the Scriptures were held, was to use some such introductory formula as 'it is written,' or 'the Scripture saith.'   It is when we discover this formula transferred to quotations from the New Testament writings that we feel ourselves to be on safe ground, in affirming that such writings had achieved a position of authority similar to that of the Hebrew Scriptures.

29.   For some considerable period it is probable that the Christian Church would have felt no need of any authoritative writings of her own.   She had the Jewish Bible, which spoke prophetically of Christ ; she had the oral tradition of the works and words of Jesus Himself ; she had the living witness of the apostles and early disciples, who came and went from church to church, imparting fresh information about the Master, together with words of life and hope : and, in view of the immediate return of Christ from Heaven, she needed no more than these. When Christians met together for worship in each other's houses, their form of service would have followed the model of the synagogue ; prayer, the reading of passages from the Law and the Prophets, words of exhortation (and the sermon would have been a feature of great importance when an apostle was present); and this would generally have been followed by a repetition of the Lord's Supper.

Need of Christian Scriptures not born at once.

30. Nevertheless in the natural course of events
definitely Christian writings were gradually,
throughout this period, coming into existence.   Here an unknown believer was
setting down, perhaps for his own edification, a collection
of certain of the utterances of Jesus ; there another was
inditing, for the comfort and assurance of his brethren,
a series of visions, in the manner of the well-known
Jewish apocalyptic writings ; and there again an apostle
was writing letters to several churches he had founded,
to help them in the difficulties and dangers they were
called upon to face.   The circumstances of the origin of
the different writings we possess we shall consider at
a later stage, under the heading of literary criticism.
Here we are concerned only with the question of the
collection and appreciation of these writings ; and in this
connection it is important to notice how they were all of
them strictly of an occasional character.   That is to
say, they were written to meet the needs of the moment,
and in entire unconsciousness that they would have any
value for posterity, or would ever survive to attain to the
status of inspired and authoritative documents.   That
the various books speedily attained a great popularity,
and were widely diffused throughout the Christian
Church, is due to a number of causes we shall specify ;
but it was clearly not contemplated by their authors.

31.   In the case of a Pauline epistle it is not difficult
Causes which
led to preserva-
tion of such
writings. to picture to ourselves the circumstances
which conduced to its preservation.   In the
first place, the letter as a rule was addressed
not to an individual but to a community, or to a
community through the individual ; and it dealt with
problems in which the very life of the community was at

stake, and in which therefore every member was directly
(a) Public   concerned. In some cases the letter was an
reading.   answer to questions which had been put to
the writer by sorely-perplexed officials; and in every
case it would have been regarded as possessing an
authority peculiar to one who had himself founded and
directed the church to which he was writing. A letter of
this character must certainly have been read in public;
and the most fitting occasion would have been when the
community was assembled for worship. What would
have been more natural than that, in the absence of
the apostle, his written words of instruction, warning
or exhortation, should have been read in the place of the
sermon? Moreover, such a letter once read was not
straightway consigned to oblivion. It would have been
re-read on further occasions of public worship, studied
and pondered; until the original document had become
frayed and torn. Then one of the community, for his
own behoof if not for all, would have made a transcription
of it. Some of these letters were intended from the
outset for a wider audience. In cases where two or more
churches were near neighbours, and the problems with
which they had to deal were similar or identical, the
author expressed a wish that his letters should be inter-
changed; and this would almost certainly have implied,
not that any church parted with its original document,
but that copies were multiplied, and that the different
churches thus acquired the first foundations of a library
of Christian writings.

When death removed, one by one, the apostolic
founders of the churches, and by the dropping out of the
immediate disciples of Jesus the connecting links with
His age were gradually disappearing, it was inevitable

that the authority of the Twelve and their circle should
have rapidly increased rather than diminished. In proportion as the voice of the living witness was silenced,
and it was no more possible for men to drink in from the
mouth of the preacher what had been seen and handled of
the Word of Life, so reverence for the written documents
which the first disciples had left behind them increased,
and the books themselves began to assume an importance
they had not previously possessed. If they were not yet
regarded as being sacred, at least they had a place to
themselves apart from other writings in the affections
of Christians ; for they represented the earliest and most
authoritative witness existing to the sacred truths they
cherished. It was thus that writings, which had originally
been publicly read because of the peculiar character of
their destination, came to be read at public worship with
increasing regularity, not in place of the preaching, but
side by side with it ; as supplying the norm of Christian
experience and doctrine, which the preaching could only
supplement and develop. In this way the writings were
already on the high road to canonicity, owing to the fact
that their public reading at once introduced a rivalry,
and challenged a comparison with the Old Testament
Scriptures, the reading of which formed a part of Divine
Service.

It was when this enhanced value was put upon the
(*b*) Collections Christian writings that individual churches,
of writings. or their representatives, set themselves to
collect what they could lay their hands upon of the
writings of their author, other than the epistle they
originally possessed. Communication between the various
churches was, as we gather from the New Testament
writings themselves as well as from other early Christian

literature, constant and close; and the means of communication were made easy by the organised services of the empire. Thus it would not have been difficult for any single church to learn of the existence of an epistle in the hands of another church, and to possess itself of a copy. The letters to the churches of a single province would naturally have been first collected; and these early groups would have later been combined, as the pecuniary resources of a community allowed. Ephesians, Colossians and Philemon formed an Asiatic collection; 1 and 2 Thessalonians and Philippians a Macedonian. Within the first group Galatians would shortly have been gathered; while 1 and 2 Corinthians would have fallen to the second. It is, of course, probable that St Paul may have written other letters of a like character to those we possess; and it is equally probable that, had these been preserved, they would have been reckoned as canonical in a like degree. But we must allow that in certain cases an autograph would have perished, through the wear of constant use, before any reader had sufficiently appraised its value as to lead to a transcription being made.

32. The case of the four Gospels is rather different. It appears that individual Christians, probably those whose task was that of preaching and instructing, the prophets and evangelists, must at an early period have made for themselves collections of the sayings of Jesus, together perhaps with certain incidents in His ministry, possibly as a basis for the oral instruction they had to impart. None of these collections would have covered precisely the same ground, or contained the same material. It would have been natural that, in course of time, a demand should have arisen for a more

<small>Case of the Gospels.</small>

complete and authoritative account of those things which all desired to know, for a sort of biography of Him whom all worshipped.   Especially in the absence of those who had companied with Him, it would have been felt that a written narrative of His teaching and of the events of His earthly life, compiled in an orderly and intelligible fashion, was a thing to be desired.   Accordingly attempts were made to meet this demand ; and amongst them appeared our own four Gospels.   Such writings were certain of immediate acceptance, and would at once have obtained the dignity of being publicly read, both because their theme was of such high importance, and also because they supplied a want which had been realised. More especially would they have been certain of success when they were known to contain, one of them the recollections of St Peter, as did St Mark, and another the Gospel tradition committed to St Paul, as did St Luke. We shall have more to say about the history and composition of the Gospels under the heading of literary criticism ; but we may remark here that, although our four Gospels were amongst the latest of the New Testament writings to appear, it was considerations such as those we have enumerated which would have led to their obtaining the crown of canonicity in advance of all the rest.

33.   Enough has been said to indicate the sort of circumstances which conduced to the preservation of our New Testament books by the early Church.   It has also become clear that the determining factor, in the causes which led to their being treated as sacred, was their introduction for public reading into the services of the Christian communities, where they naturally assumed, in

The processes of selection, and existence of other writings.

course of time, a footing of equality with the Old Testament Canon. We must now stay to enquire whether, besides the books we possess in our New Testament, there were others produced in early Christian circles which were not so admitted to the Canon ; whether, that is to say, there is evidence of any selective process, and if so what it amounted to. When we come to discuss the composition of the Gospels, we shall learn that certain evangelistic records and collections previously existing were absorbed into those we possess. But in addition to these we learn that other Gospels were in circulation ; that 'according to the Hebrews,' for instance, and another 'according to the Egyptians.' Of these we know practically nothing ; but a fragment of a so called 'Gospel of St Peter' has recently come to light, and is found to exhibit heretical tendencies. So far as we can gather from what is left of it, it would seem that it is based on our own Gospels, and is not independent of them. But the remarkable thing for us to notice is that, from the earliest times, our four Gospels appear to have reigned supreme. For while, on the one hand, the references found in patristic literature to others than the canonical Gospels (in the writings of Justin Martyr and Clement of Alexandria in particular) are relatively infrequent; on the other hand, in the opinion of some scholars (cp. Souter, *Text and Canon of the N.T.* p. 161), the 'Teaching of the Twelve Apostles,' a Christian book which may be dated circ. 110 A.D., already refers to our four as a collection, under the single title of 'the Gospel.' In other words, books which were so speedily conceded a position of unquestioned superiority, cannot have encountered any serious competition from other works of a similar character.

That there was in existence, at different times, an abundance of Christian writings of an occasional character, letters of St Paul and other leaders of the churches, and perhaps a few apocalypses, is most probable; but circumstances, amongst which we must place the ready appreciation by their readers of their spiritual force, and the recognised authority of the writer, did not conspire to their preservation. Only one document belonging to the 1st century has reached us, other than those which have found their way into the Canon; namely the so called first epistle of Clement of Rome to the Corinthians; and the simple force and beauty of this production justifies the discrimination which saved it from destruction. But the process of book-making had not yet begun in Christian circles; and in no separate locality could the number of competing documents have been at any time large. On the whole, we may probably say that, while the preservation of certain writings depended so much upon what were, humanly speaking, fortuitous circumstances, there was no distinct and conscious principle, or method, of selection to be observed.

(a) But little selection in earliest times.

In addition to the Jewish Scriptures it would appear that Christian circles gave much attention to the later Jewish apocryphal and other writings; especially to those of an apocalyptic character, which harmonised with their ideas of the speedy return of Christ and the end of the present age. Witness to this is forthcoming from the fact that so many of these writings have clearly been edited by Christian hands, receiving additions which would be likely to make them the more welcome to Christian readers. The book known as 2 Esdras, and 'The

(b) The motives towards book-making.

Testaments of the Twelve Patriarchs' are instances of this; but a more striking illustration is the recently discovered 'Teaching of the Twelve Apostles,' which is a Christian work founded upon an older Jewish book known as 'The Two Ways.' It is perhaps legitimate to infer two things from these facts. First, that the reading of Gospels and Epistles at public services had whetted the appetites of the Christian communities for a wider spiritual pasture to wander in, while as yet no New Testament Canon was dreamed of. If this were so, what could be more natural than that their thoughts should turn first to the Jewish apocalypses, edited by Christian hands, since the Church lived in daily expectation of the return of their Master? And when we recollect that Christian communities read the Old Testament in the LXX version, and that the books of our Apocrypha were already attached to that version, and were for that reason regarded by Christians as in some sense canonical; we shall see that the step to be taken was not a long one. But, second, this novel literary activity, the editing of Jewish works, was very probably the commencement of the new era of book-making; for, especially when the last and irretrievable breach with the Jewish synagogues was effected, the Christian circles would have become fully conscious of their need of a literature of their own. Thus, in the strange book known as 'The Shepherd of Hermas,' which may be dated about 150 A.D., we have an apocalypse of wholly Christian origin.

Now a condition of great difficulty and perplexity would have been produced by this intro-
(c) Idea of Canon emerging, and limitation of writings. duction of a number of works of very diverse character into the public reading of the Church; for, with the apocalypses,

the flood-gates would have been opened to let in gradually Acts of Apostles and Martyrs, Gospels of the Infancy, and so forth. While certain books were on the high road to being recognised as canonical, what was to be said of this mass of other literature ? Was a similar reverence to be accorded to it, or should a line of distinction be drawn ? Gradually questions of this kind led to the formation of a method or principle of criticism ; for the first time a conscious selection came into play. It was felt that it was desirable to check a growing licence in the choice of books suitable for public reading, and that only those should be allowed which were of the highest value for edification. Other books came to be classified as apocryphal (secret); useful, that is, for private study but not for public reading. In this way arose a tendency to reduce the allowed books to a fixed quantity, and in course of time to admit into their number only those which were thought to be very ancient, and apostolic in authorship. And thus, too, was evolved the later theory that the canonical books were written as Scripture by apostolic men, and handed over by them for the guidance, and to the safe-keeping, of the Church.

34. But during this process of the limitation and constitution of the Canon, it was inevitable that there should have been felt a certain dubiousness with regard to the claims of certain amongst the competing books. On the one hand there would have been a number of writings whose right to be received into the Canon would never have been disputed ; and another large class of works whose rejection was certain from the outset. But, on the other hand, between these two classes, there would have been two smaller groups of documents

Dubiety entertained about certain books.

about which a considerable degree of uncertainty obtained; those which were at the first admitted, provisionally, and afterwards excluded; and those which were at the first excluded, but afterwards admitted. And as a matter of fact our evidence enables us to distinguish some at least of these books. To the first class, of writings which attained a temporary canonicity, belong 'The Teaching of the Twelve Apostles,' A.D. 110, 'The 1st Epistle to the Corinthians' of Clement of Rome, A.D. 95, 'The Epistle of Barnabas,' in its present form, probably A.D. 130, 'The Shepherd of Hermas,' A.D. 150, 'The Apocalypse of Peter,' A.D. 145, 'The Acts of Paul,' A.D. 160, and the so-called '2nd Epistle to the Corinthians,' wrongly attributed to Clement of Rome, A.D. 140. To the second class, of writings which were not at first admitted to the Canon, belong James, 2 Peter, 2 and 3 John, Jude, and Hebrews.

35. The testimony to the existence and use of our

Unequal history of Canon in different localities.

canonical books opens with the 1st Epistle of Clement of Rome, in which allusions to several of the writings may be discovered. This testimony is continued, on the one side by heretical writers, whose external evidence to the value of books used by the Church is of great importance; and on the other side by Christian fathers, from Justin Martyr onwards. It would not do otherwise than invest our subject with tediousness if we were to attempt, in the space at our disposal, the task of reproducing here the testimony to the various books, or collections of books, author by author. But a few remarks should be made upon the character of this testimony. In the first place, if a particular author does not happen to cite any one or more of our canonical books, we have no right to

B. 10

conclude, either that those books were not yet in existence or that they were not already regarded as of equal authority with the books from which he does quote. On the other hand, when we find that our canonical writings are quoted almost to the exclusion of other Christian books, or with a respect which obviously places them in a superior category, we are justified in seeing a reflection of a certain selective process in action, guided it may be very largely by a sort of instinctive spiritual judgment. And on these grounds we may with some confidence believe that, though some works may have been lost which posterity would have accorded a place in the Canon, on the whole what was of most value in early Christian literature has been preserved for us. Again, we must not suppose that this selective process was everywhere the same, nor that it proceeded in every locality with a similar momentum. The scattered communities of east and west would not, in the earlier days, have possessed all the books ultimately submitted to the judgment of the whole Church. In one locality a particular book would have been treated as authoritative, while in another it was still regarded with some uncertainty. In a remote church a certain writing would have been esteemed very highly, until the opinion of wider circles came to correct this erroneous judgment. Thus in widely separated countries the selection went on more or less independently at first ; but as the channels of communication between distant communities produced a closer intimacy, and the Church as a whole achieved a higher degree of cohesion and unity, so there was ever brought to bear upon the problem a wider exercise of discrimination, and a deeper insight, which eventually resulted in a balance of opinion. In this way a Canon of Scripture was completed before such a Canon could be officially promulgated, and without the conscious operation of any distinct standard or principle of canonicity. And, once completed to the number of our present books, the Canon was automatically closed ; for no later productions could hope to win for themselves anything like an universal acceptance, when it came to be seen that the Canon was limited (in our opinion, only roughly ; but, in the opinion of the Church of the 4th century, with much greater precision) to works of the apostolic age, if not of apostolic authorship.

36. It will be perceived that, the material being

Gradual unanimity of opinion, and stages by which it was reached.

such as we have described, it is not an easy matter to delimit any definite stages in the growth of the New Testament Canon, or to say confidently what writings were, by practical agreement, treated as inspired at any particular date in the history of that growth. We may follow up the quotations from a particular book in patristic writings, noting whether these quotations are loose or accurate, whether they are introduced with a formula used with citations from the Old Testament, and whether the book itself, and perhaps its author, is named ; and in this way we may observe the growth of a sense of value, of a feeling of inspiration and authority, in respect of such a book. We may observe what books are utilised by any particular author, the degree of preference he exhibits for them in comparison with others, and the extent of sanctity and authority he appears to attribute to them ; and of such a writer we may affirm that for him, and possibly for his readers, such was already his Canon of Scripture. But we must expect to find no universal consent in all the stages of the growth of the Canon ;

and, from what we have already said, it will be gathered
that the history of this growth was not precisely the
same in all branches of the Church. The Roman and
African churches, for instance, admitted the disputed
books to their Canon before they were accepted by the
churches of the east, of Syria and Assyria. But there
are, nevertheless, certain landmarks, more or less arbitrary in character, which may be taken conveniently to
divide the history into periods. The first of these periods
may be said to extend, roughly, to the year 170 A.D.
This period is characterised, on the whole, by an allusive
use of the New Testament books, and by looseness of
quotation. Yet a study of the writings of the period,
whether those of Churchmen or of heretics, proves that
most, if not all, of the documents were in existence and
in use ; and that many of them were already invested
with a high degree of authority. Moreover it seems clear
that, in some places, the various books had already been
formed into collections—four Gospels, and ten Pauline
epistles. And, further, the heretic Marcion, at least, was
amongst those who had formed the conception of a
Canon ; for he distinctly laid down for his followers what
books, and portions of books, were to be received, and
what rejected. The second period opens with the publication of Tatian's Diatessaron, a harmony of the four
Gospels, in 170 A.D., and closes with the death of
Tertullian in 220 A.D. This period is marked by a more
extensive, and at the same time a more exact, use of the
New Testament books in the matter of quotation. And
this in itself is evidence of an increased sense of the
religious value and authority, and therefore of the inspiration, of these books. Most of all, this comes out in
the writings of Irenaeus. It was, probably, during this

period that the Old Syriac and the Old Latin versions were made; and they must be allowed to play an important part in providing evidence of what was, and what was not, received. A comparison of these with the works of Tatian, of Irenaeus, of Clement of Alexandria and of Tertullian, which may be taken as representative of the opinions of the churches of Syria, Asia Minor, Egypt, Africa and Gaul, enables us to say with tolerable certainty what books were regarded, universally, as authoritative and inspired towards the close of the 2nd century. Our evidence would seem to assign to this rudimentary Canon the four Gospels, all the Pauline epistles with the possible exception of Philemon, the Acts, the Apocalypse, 1 Peter and 1 John. The third period commences in 220 A.D., and closes in 397 A.D. with the first conciliar promulgation of a New Testament Canon. Beyond that point it is unnecessary for us to travel. This period is distinguished by a living interest in, and much discussion of, the question of canonicity itself. It is a period which produced a great succession of profound Biblical students and scholars; Origen, Athanasius, Eusebius of Caesarea, Cyril of Jerusalem and Chrysostom, in the east; Cyprian, Jerome, Augustine, Hilary of Poitiers and Ambrose of Milan, in the west. Men such as these, both by their writings and by the lists of canonical books they themselves published, undoubtedly exercised an important influence upon the Church at large, in the formation of opinion upon the matter of the Canon; an influence which must not be under-estimated, since it was during this period that finality appears to have been reached. But, at the same time, it is surely remarkable that a close unanimity of opinion was attained without the exercise of any

disciplinary force or compulsion.   And when, at the 3rd
Council of Carthage, in the year 397 A.D., a Canon of the
New Testament Scriptures was for the first time officially
issued, a Canon which is in every respect identical with
our own, we are able to affirm that it only stereotyped or
regulated a result which had already been achieved by
other means.

37.   In treating of our third division, that of Literary
Criticism, we may first of all remind our-
selves that the questions awaiting our study
are such as these.   By whom were our
various books written, and what was the date and locality
at which they first saw the light ?   Under what circumstances were they produced, and to what class of readers
were they addressed ?   What was the manner of their
production, and were they originally the unities we
possess, or were they, some of them, compiled from other
writings, edited and revised from time to time ?   And, if
their composition was of this character, what were the
sources to which they were indebted, by whom and when
were those sources written, and who was responsible for
the task of editing them ?   Here we have a host of
related problems, the solutions of which depend upon
a combination of internal evidence, derived from a
study of the books themselves, and external evidence,
derived from what other early Christian writers have
to say about them.   A full treatment of these questions
belongs to what is commonly known as 'introduction';
and here we can only indicate the nature of some
of the principal problems, the difficulties which have
to be faced, and the probable conclusions reached by
scholars in certain cases.   It will be convenient to
begin with the epistles which are grouped together in

Problems of Literary Criticism.

our Bible under the name of St Paul, since these are, at least in certain cases, chronologically the earliest writings we possess. We shall then pass on to consider the first three Gospels, which present us with a problem similar to that of the Hexateuch in the Old Testament. From them we shall turn to the writings associated with the name of St John; and finally we shall glance in turn at each of the remaining books.

38. First, then, the Pauline epistles. There are thirteen books in our New Testament Canon definitely attributed to this apostle. For all of these the external evidence is strong in favour of St Paul being their author. They all find a place in the Muratorian Canon, a fragment of a MS belonging roughly to the year 200 A.D. and named after its first editor, Muratori. They are all of them quoted, if not distinctly named, by Irenaeus, circ. 180 A.D. And direct quotations or unmistakable allusions to all of them are found in earlier writers; in a few cases going back even to Clement of Rome, in the year 95 A.D. In short, the current of tradition is both wide and strong which would credit St Paul with these writings, a certain hesitation having been felt, apparently, about the Pastoral epistles only (i.e. 1 and 2 Timothy, Titus). Now tradition must probably be allowed considerable weight in a question of this kind, when the tradition itself is discovered to be so early and so unanimous. Moreover the evidence of the use of these writings by other Christian authors seems sufficient to cast back most, if not all, of them to the 1st century, even if it does not definitely warrant our ascription of them to St Paul. But when we have located them so early in the history of the Church, we may well ask, 'To whom, if not to

The Pauline Epistles. (a) Genuineness.

St Paul, could they possibly be attributed?' This is not to deny that there may have been others amongst the first leaders of the Church possessed of such strong religious genius; but rather we affirm that the writings, in the main, bear upon the face of them such indubitable marks of St Paul's handiwork, that to give them to another would at once label them as forgeries; and to suppose them forgeries, executed with such extraordinary skill, so near to the date of St Paul's activities, and so widely and early accepted by the Church as Pauline, is a reversal of all the probabilities of the case. For, in general, their internal evidence is also strongly in their favour. If we accept the evidence of Acts upon the character and work of St Paul, his temperament, his doctrines, his controversies and so forth, we find that the epistles not only reflect the characteristics and circumstances which meet us in the biography that work gives us, but also that they may, with confidence in the majority of cases, be fitted into the historical framework which it provides.

Before we go on to survey the ground in more detail, we may here interpolate a remark upon the manner in which the epistles were written, according to the evidence which they themselves provide. It seems that St Paul's habit was, as a general rule, to dictate to an amanuensis. In Rom. xvi. 22 we discover that his amanuensis was Tertius. Reasons for this custom may have been, the affliction of the eyes from which we know he suffered, and possibly the roughness of his hands produced by his trade of tent-making. These would explain the clumsy and uncouth handwriting which was characteristic of his style, when, as in Gal. vi. 11—18, he took the pen into his own

(b) Dictation, and Short-hand.

hand. Nevertheless it was usual for him to append a greeting to most of his epistles, as a man will sign his name to a type-written letter (cp. 2 Thess. iii. 17, 18; 1 Cor. xvi. 21—24; Col. iv. 18); and it was necessary that he should himself write his bond in Philemon 19. Now the art of shorthand is no modern invention; and there not only exists evidence of its use in the writings of classical antiquity, but certain specimens of it have recently come to light. It may therefore be considered probable that an author who dictated so largely as did St Paul, would have utilised when possible the services of one who had a knowledge of shorthand writing.

And this supposition is to some extent corroborated (c) Differences by the evidence of the epistles themselves; in style. for it helps to explain certain differences in style which are otherwise very perplexing. Thus, with regard to such epistles as 1 Corinthians and Galatians, we may feel that the fervid language and abrupt sentences indicate that the letters were taken down and despatched exactly as St Paul spoke them. Others, such as Romans, may indicate a careful revision of the somewhat elaborate argument. And with regard to yet others, Colossians and Ephesians in particular, we may be inclined to believe that St Paul contented himself with discussing the main points of his doctrine with his scribe, explaining the views he wished to expound, and then leaving him, perhaps Timothy, to work up the epistles from a series of notes he had taken down.

The thirteen epistles appear to fall into four groups, (d) Four between each of which there elapsed an groups. interval of a few years. The first group is (i.) 1 and 2 Thessa- constituted by the two to the Thessalonians. lonians. The eschatological teaching which they have in common indicates an early date for these; and the modifications of this teaching found in the second, together with its reference to a former epistle (2 Thess. ii. 15), indicate that we have the letters in their proper order. A comparison of the internal evidence (e.g. 1 Thess. iii. 1, 2) with the narrative of Ac. xvii, xviii, suggests that 1 Thessalonians was written at Corinth on St Paul's first visit to that city ; and, according to the chronological scheme which is now very generally accepted, it may be dated A.D. 53. And, if so, then 2 Thessalonians probably followed, also from Corinth, in the following year.

To the second group belong 1 and 2 Corinthians, (ii.) 1 Corinthians. Galatians, and Romans. Of these, 1 Corinthians appears to have been written at Ephesus, probably in the year A.D. 56 (cp. 1 Cor. xvi. 8, 19), previous to a second visit to Corinth (1 Cor. xvi. 3—6 ; cp. Ac. xix. 1, 21, 22) ; though we gather that the uproar raised by Demetrius had the effect of modifying the author's plans (Ac. xx. 1—3, 16). In 2 Corinthians we encounter a literary problem of considerable interest. The reader cannot fail to notice that, in passing from the ninth to the tenth chapter, the whole character and tone of the epistle changes ; there is an abrupt transition to a great severity, with nothing to account for it in the preceding portion, and which indeed is out of place after 2 Cor. vii. 6, 7. This suggests that the epistle is not a unity, but is compounded of two separate letters, which the accident of contiguity has woven into one. If this be so, then there is much plausibility in the theory that 2 Cor. x—xiii represents a third letter, intermediate between 1 Corinthians and 2 Cor. i—ix. In support of this, we may notice that 2 Cor. vii. 8, 9 cannot very well refer to 1 Cor. ; but it is very adequately descriptive of 2 Cor. x—xiii. And thus, too, 2 Cor. x—xiii may very well be the epistle referred to in 2 Cor. ii. 4, iii. 1 ; though we must bear in mind that already a former letter has been mentioned in 1 Cor. v. 9. From 2 Cor. xii. 14, xiii. 1, 2, we gather that the apostle, who is now projecting his third visit, must have paid a brief second visit to Corinth not recorded in Acts, when he met with the treatment which called for the severe tone of 2 Cor. x—xiii. And we infer that 2 Cor. i—ix was written on receipt of the news that his letter had wrought a change, and with the satisfaction of knowing he could now visit his converts with more of happiness. It seems that 2 Cor. i—ix was written from Macedonia, shortly after the events which led to St Paul's leaving Ephesus (cp. 2 Cor. i. 8—10; Ac. xix. 23—xx. 1); therefore 2 Cor. x—xiii must have been written at Ephesus shortly before those events. And if 1 Cor. was written in A.D. 56, then 2 Cor. x—xiii and i—ix must have been written early in the year A.D. 57 (cp. Ac. xx. 16). The other two epistles of this group are closely related to each other in respect of their subject-matter, which is the errors and personal hostility of a certain party amongst the Jewish converts to Christianity ; and that, together with a good deal of verbal similarity between the two, may probably be taken to indicate that they were not far removed in the dates of their production. An interesting question arises

Galatians. in connection with the destination of Galatians ; the problem being whether Galatia indicates a district in the north of Asia Minor, colonised by Celts from Gaul, or a Roman province of that name, which included the districts and towns in Asia Minor visited by St Paul on his first and second missionary

journeys. Sundry reasons of great weight have led most
scholars to adopt the latter view, and to understand by
the Galatians the Christian churches of Antioch, Iconium,
Derbe and Lystra. We conclude from Gal. iv. 13 that
St Paul had already visited these churches twice (i.e. the
visits of Ac. xiii, xiv, and xvi. 1—5), and from Gal. i. 6
that no great period of time had elapsed since the first
visit. But in view of the difference in the thought of the
epistle and the circumstances which called for it, we are
bound to place it some while after those to the Thessalonians. Thus we shall probably not be far wrong if we
suppose St Paul wrote it at Ephesus in A.D. 56, shortly
before 1 Corinthians. In the case of Romans

Romans.
a literary difficulty has to be faced, about
which scholars have not as yet reached any widely
accepted solution. It is concerned with the last two
chapters of the epistle. The first point which strikes the
reader as strange is that these chapters provide no less
than three separate conclusions, at xv. 33, xvi. 20, and
xvi. 27. The next that, when as yet St Paul had never
visited Rome, it is curious that he should possess so large
a circle of personal friends in the city; a fact which
appears to contradict the evidence of the main body of
the epistle, in which he seems to be writing to strangers.
In addition to difficulties of this kind, the researches of
scholars have revealed several interesting facts, of which
we may note two here. One is that, according to the
evidence of some ancient writers, there existed in the
2nd century a recension of the epistle which omitted
almost the whole of these two chapters, namely xv. 1 to
xvi. 23. The other, that one ancient MS omits the
words 'in Rome' in Ro. i. 7 and 15. It is possible that
these facts may be explained on the hypothesis that what

we now call an 'epistle to the Romans' was originally intended for a wider audience; and that, copies of it being sent to the various churches, the blank spaces in i. 7, 15, were intended to be filled in with the names of those churches; while the majority of MSS which have reached us have descended from the copy sent to Rome. This is a phenomenon which will meet us in the case of Ephesians, where it is clearly established. And, if this is so, then the last two chapters (exclusive of xvi. 25—27 which was the original conclusion) would have formed a covering letter to one of these other churches, not Rome; and possibly we may conclude, from the fact that so many friends are mentioned by name, and especially from the inclusion of Prisca and Aquila (xvi. 3), that the church was that of Ephesus, where St Paul had resided for so long a time. Such is a plausible theory; but this is not the place to discuss it. We may, however, argue from xv. 25, 26 that the epistle was written in Achaia, and possibly at Corinth, on St Paul's second (or, in view of 2 Cor. x—xiii, his third) visit to that city (cp. Ac. xx. 2; Ro. xv. 19); and that would place it early in A.D. 57, after 2 Cor. i—ix.

The third group of epistles consists of Colossians, (iii.) Difficulties. Ephesians, Philippians and Philemon. With regard to this group very considerable doubts have been entertained as to whether St Paul was indeed their author. These doubts are, indeed, far from being dispelled; but of recent years the opinion of many competent judges has been inclining more and more towards the ascription of them to him. The main objections urged against their Pauline authorship are, first, that they exhibit a great advance in points of Christian doctrine; second, that they appear to deal with heresies

which did not arise until a later period ; third, that we
miss in them the vehement style which is so characteristic
of the Apostle ; and fourth, that they show a much wider
acquaintance with the Greek language.   But answers to
each of these objections are forthcoming.   The first and
last may perhaps be accounted for by the lapse of time
since the writing of Romans ; the third by the circumstances of St Paul's imprisonment and his increasing
age ; and the second by denying (as some think we have
good ground for doing) that the heresies are of a later
type.   But, in addition, we may also surmise that some
of the peculiarities are, as a matter of fact, due to the
amanuensis whom St Paul employed.   Philippians, it
may be stated, does not present us with the same degree
of perplexity as encounters us in Colossians and Ephesians.

Philemon.
The mention of Archippus and Onesimus
in Philemon 1, 11, associates this, the only
strictly personal letter by St Paul we possess, with Colossians (cp. iv. 17, 9), and makes it clear that Philemon
lived at Colossae.   It is therefore probable that both
were written at the same time, and sent by the same
messenger, Tychicus (Col. iv. 7).   Colossians,

Colossians.
as we gather from its pages, was written at
Rome, during St Paul's imprisonment, and is generally
assigned to the year A.D. 62.   The first feature to attract

Ephesians.
our attention in respect of Ephesians is that
quite half the epistle is almost identical,
word for word, with that to the Colossians.   Another
point to be noticed is that two very important MSS, ℵ
and B, omit the words 'at Ephesus' in the opening
verse.   And, still further, it is very remarkable that, in
writing to a church which he knew so intimately, St Paul
should have omitted to greet any of his friends by name;

for there are no greetings in Ephesians. It is therefore most probable that Ephesians was originally a circular letter, intended for Ephesus amongst other churches, but not exclusively for her. The heretic Marcion knew the epistle as that 'To the Laodiceans,' which suggests that his copy read 'Laodicea' where ours reads 'Ephesus.' And it is quite possible that the epistle referred to in Col. iv. 16, which the Colossians expected to receive 'from Laodicea,' was our Ephesians. The striking similarity between Ephesians and Colossians would be explained by the fact that they were written at the same time, that they were written by the same scribe—possibly Timothy, and that they dealt with the same subjects. Thus we may date Ephesians as written at Rome in the year A.D. 62,

Philippians. and despatched by Tychicus. Philippians was probably written later in the same year, shortly before the conclusion of St Paul's imprisonment; for the whole letter, especially such passages as i. 20—24, ii. 17, 24, exhibits the calm expectancy of one who knew that the end of his captivity must be near, but who knew not whether the issue would be death or freedom.

In the fourth and last group, that of the Pastoral **(iv.) Difficul-** epistles, we are confronted by certain serious **ties.** difficulties. In quite early days certain writers rejected them as being un-Pauline. They did not so soon find admittance into the Canon; their right being disputed, probably, because their authorship was regarded as uncertain. And in modern days it has been objected to them, first, that their language and style is not that of St Paul; second, that they reflect a development in Church order and discipline such as St Paul could never have lived to see; third, that they deal with heretical doctrines which sprang into existence later than his day; and fourth, that the biography of St Paul in Acts provides us with no historical situation into which we can fit them. And it must be admitted that there is much cogency in these objections. And yet there is a great similarity of spirit and ideas, between them and the recognised epistles of St Paul; and it is hardly conceivable that they can have been forgeries. It is far more plausible to suppose that, in them, we have authentic letters of St Paul, which have been worked over by the hand of a later editor to bring them into touch with new conditions in the life of the Church. But about this we can say nothing certainly. If we are prepared to accept them as originally Pauline, then we are driven to conjecture that St Paul was liberated from prison after the writing of Philippians, that he engaged in a second period of ministerial activity, and that he suffered a further term of imprisonment before his martyrdom. There is no historical evidence for this conjecture; but it cannot be regarded as impossible. If, then, we adopt 1 Timothy, which was written in Macedonia (i. 3; iii. 14, 15), may be dated about A.D. 64; while Titus, which exhibits many points of similarity to it, may be given to the same locality and time. On the other hand, 2 Timothy is written from a second imprisonment at Rome, apparently very shortly before St Paul's death (iv. 16, 6), and perhaps belongs to the year A.D. 65.

1 Timothy.
Titus.

2 Timothy.

39. We leave the Pauline epistles, and turn to the first three of our Canonical Gospels. A marked difference in the treatment of our Lord's life is plain to the most casual reader, between that of the first three Gospels and the fourth; and

The Synoptic Gospels.

consequently the first three have come to be spoken of as the Synoptic Gospels ; those, that is, which exhibit in their contents and attitude to their subject a common view. The questions raised in regard to these three are not only concerned with their authorship and the place and date of their production, but still more with considerations of the sources whence they derived their information, of the manner and history of their composition, and of the relations existing between them. This it is which is known as the Synoptic Problem, of which we must proceed to give some account.

40. First of all our attention is drawn to the very striking resemblances which each Gospel bears to the other two. If we take St Mark as the basis of our investigation, and institute a careful comparison of its text with those of St Matthew and St Luke, this resemblance at once becomes obvious. Not only is it true that almost the whole of Mark is to be found either in both the others, or in one or other of them separately; but the order and arrangement of Mark are, with a few exceptions, adhered to by both, or by one when the other departs from them ; and, further, except for an editorial revision of which we shall presently speak, both Matthew and Luke reproduce in large measure the very phrases and words which Mark uses, either separately or in company.

Synoptic Problem.
(a) Likenesses.

This phenomenon, it seems, can only be held to point to one thing ; namely that Matthew and Luke both had Mark before them, and both incorporated it, to the extent we observe, in their own works. It is indeed probable that it was not precisely our Mark which these others utilised, but rather an original document which underwent some revision subsequent

(β) Use of Mark.

to this usage. But a discussion of the problems thus suggested would lead us too far afield; and it is sufficient, here, to notice the very substantial dependence of the first and third Gospels upon the second.

But, in the second place, our attention is drawn to the marked differences between the three Gospels. When we have reached, by the aid of textual criticism, a very close approximation to the autographs, we do not find that any of the differences tend to disappear. Nor are they to be accounted for by the natural errors of a copyist, in the use which Matthew and Luke have made of Mark. They spread too widely and go too deep for that. They may, in the main, be tabulated under four heads, as follows. In the first place, we notice that Mark's Gospel is very limited in its scope, being confined to an account of the ministry in Galilee and the last week in Jerusalem. To this both Matthew and Luke make large additions. Matthew has a mass of teachings and parables, Luke a number of incidents, to incorporate; and, in order to make room for them, they are compelled to reject certain material provided by Mark. We may recall, in this connection, that the size of a papyrus roll may have necessitated an economy of this kind. But, in the second place, there occur in both certain alterations in Mark's order of events. Luke was obliged to rearrange Mark's material, in order to find suitable places for the introduction of his fresh information; but he is careful not to dislocate Mark's order at all seriously. Matthew, however, prefers to group together teachings and incidents which are similar in character, regardless of chronological arrangement; and thus he is found to disturb Mark's order more seriously than does Luke. And we may also notice this about

(γ) Differences.

Matthew, that he shows a predilection for a numerical arrangement in his groups, an artificiality dear to the Jewish mind, which distinguishes his Gospel widely from the careful historical composition of Luke, and still more widely from the naïve memoirs of Mark. And, further, both Matthew and Luke, each in his own way and for the sake of compression, pare away from Mark a good deal of those picturesque touches which are not strictly necessary to the narrative ; they improve the style of his language at various points; they correct some of his historical and geographical inaccuracies ; they tone down, from a feeling of reverence, the realism of Mark's portraiture of our Lord ; and they expand the suggestion of the hostility of the Jews towards Him.

These are some of the principal differences; and they (δ) Independence of Matthew and Luke. are only explicable by the assumption of two things. The first is that both Matthew and Luke used Mark independently of each other, and that, in using him, they did not scruple to edit his text very freely. The second is that both Matthew and Luke drew largely upon other sources of information ; and, in respect of Luke, he himself tells us that this was his practice. Can we go further, and give any account (ε) Source known as Q. of these other sources? We have, in the first place, to notice that there is a large measure of agreement between Matthew and Luke in passages which they do not derive from Mark. In the opinion of scholars, the two evangelists have drawn a great part of this material from an original document now lost to us, which for convenience is known as Q (from the German 'Quelle' = source): and it is one of the chief tasks of literary criticism to determine what was the character and contents of Q. If we may conclude with some critics that Q was, in the main, a collection of parables and teachings, and not a narrative of the life of Jesus, then it is possible to reconstruct from our two Gospels a fairly complete and continuous writing, which may approximate very nearly to what Q was. But in this case some of the narrative portions of the two Gospels must be traced to another source. The reason for thinking that Q was of the character described is to some extent based upon the opinion that Matthew must have used, as one of his sources, a lost collection of the sayings of Jesus, ascribed to Matthew by tradition, and said to have been written in Aramaic; though it would doubtless have been translated into Greek before it could have been used by our evangelists. The matter ascribed to Q is, according to the tendency we have noticed in him, collected by Matthew into groups; while in Luke it is freely dispersed through his narrative. And, judging from Luke's more careful preservation of Mark's order, we are justified in our presumption that he has more faithfully given us the order of Q. At the same time, from the differences existing in these passages between the two evangelists, we gather that they meted out to Q the same treatment they accorded to Mark.

(ς) Other sources. With regard to other sources, we can say nothing. Both Matthew and Luke have passages which appear in their own Gospels alone; and, while some of these may have been drawn independently from Q, it is clear that others had a different origin. Luke probably made more use of written documents, and Matthew of oral sources of information.

41. But what are we to say of the authorship of the three Gospels as we now possess them? It is convenient, in answering this question,

Dates and Authorship.

to take Luke first.   This Gospel is the first part of a
(a) **Luke.**   larger work; and, taken in connection with
                      Acts, a great many reasons may be adduced
in confirmation of the tradition which ascribes it to
St Luke himself.   There is the fact, for instance, that the
Gospel exhibits certain characteristics of St Paul's teaching, and the Acts makes St Luke his fellow-traveller;
and again, that the Gospel contains in many places
the technical language of medicine, and St Paul speaks
of St Luke as a physician; and once more, that the
Gospel shows a better acquaintance with Greek than
does Matthew, while Acts represents St Luke as being a
Gentile.   The Acts ends abruptly about the year 62 A.D.;
consequently the Gospel must fall at a later date than
that.   A number of separate considerations lead some
scholars to assign it to about 70–72 A.D.; but, beyond
suggesting the likelihood of Asia Minor, we are not yet
in a position to say where it was written.   Now, since
(β) **Mark.**   St Luke made Mark the basis of his own
                      Gospel, it is obvious that Mark was the
earlier of the two.   Again, there is no reason to discredit
the tradition which ascribed it to St Mark.   We may
observe that the Gospel was evidently intended for
Gentile readers; and tradition has it that St Peter in his
dealings with Gentiles utilised St Mark as his interpreter.
Moreover, the Gospel confines itself to the Galilean
ministry and the last week at Jerusalem; and tradition
says that St Mark wrote the recollections of St Peter,
who was associated with our Lord mainly in Galilee.
And, further, we know that St Mark was with St Paul in
Rome, whither tradition also sends St Peter.   We have,
therefore, good reason for surmising that Mark was
written at Rome about the year 65 A.D.   The question

of Matthew is more difficult. It was evidently intended

(γ) **Matthew.** for Jewish readers, and we shall probably be right in supposing it to have been written in Palestine. We have seen that it was not the work of St Matthew, though it may have been indebted to St Matthew's 'Sayings of Jesus' in a Greek dress, and so have come by its name. There are good reasons for assigning a later date to it than to Luke; and perhaps some year between 75 and 80 A.D. would not be wide of the mark. It seems clear that it very quickly won its way to a popularity above that of Luke, even in the Gentile Church; and this may be due to the fact that it was consciously compiled for liturgical purposes. In this case we should probably speak not of one author, but of several; or, rather, of a number of editors who revised the Gospel from time to time.

42. Out of the Gospels there arise several literary

Historical Problems. problems of very great interest and importance, which it is impossible to touch upon here, though we may enumerate a few of them. The sources of the chapters in Luke and Matthew concerned with the Infancy are a very obscure and perplexing subject; the relations of the different members of that collection of teachings, which goes by the name of the Sermon on the Mount, is another; the history and origins of the apocalyptic discourses is yet another. But behind these literary problems are others of still more far-reaching importance, which yet depend for their solution very largely upon the literary evidence. Here again we must be content merely to indicate a few of these, without attempting in any way to discuss them. What degree of credibility belongs to each of the three Synoptic Gospels? If, in general, Mark is more trustworthy than

Luke or Matthew, and Luke than Matthew, yet where
any two are at variance, or (say) Matthew alone records
something upon which the others are silent, may it not
be that the least trustworthy may yet preserve a more
authentic tradition? Has Q an absolute value, especially
where it has the support of Mark? But, going behind
the documents, which after all are based upon oral
tradition; to what extent are we justified in reposing confidence in the memories of uneducated men, ignorant of
the first principles of collecting and weighing evidence,
in an age when fact and fancy were not ordinarily at all
clearly distinguished, and when tradition very quickly
took to itself the elements of myth? And, further, if the
reliability of the very doings of our Lord, and of the
main events in His life, must be canvassed; what are we
to say about His teaching? Can we be sure that we
have His actual words, when we remember that we have
only a Greek rendering of what was spoken in Aramaic,
and that recorded many years after the words left His
lips? All these are matters of the gravest importance,
to which the Biblical scholar is bound to give his most
earnest attention.

43. We now pass on to the Johannine writings; by
Johannine which we imply the fourth Gospel, the three
Literature. Epistles bearing the name of St John, and
the Revelation which has often been ascribed to him.
(a) 4th Gospel. The fourth Gospel presents us with the
(i.) Difficulties. most difficult and the most severely con-
tested problem of the New Testament. It is very widely
separated, in the treatment of its subject, from the
Synoptic Gospels. It is not content merely to relate
the incidents of our Lord's life, but it goes on to interpret
the facts to religious experience, and invests the whole

history with a deep spiritual significance.   It betrays
a definite theological purpose, and its presentation of the
history is coloured by that point of view.   It incorporates
long discourses which are quite foreign to the manner of
our Lord in the pages of the Synoptists, and which are
full of new and profound thought.   The style, too, is
somewhat controversial; the author wages war against
erroneous opinions, and he exhibits a strong sense of
indignation against the Jews, whose hostility to the
Master he develops far beyond the point to which the
Synoptists take it.   Moreover, a comparison with the
pages of the first three Gospels brings out many apparent
contradictions and inconsistencies, as, for instance, a three
years' ministry in place of one covering only a single
year; and reveals many omissions of great importance,
such as the institution of the Lord's Supper.   And yet
undoubtedly the Gospel claims to be historical, and is no
mere allegory.   If it is chiefly preoccupied with great
spiritual truths, it bases these upon the facts of history;
it appeals to the whole course and tenour of our Lord's
earthly life as the warrant for the faith and living
experience of the Christian communities.   But is it
possible, nevertheless, to treat it as sober history?   Can
we credit the claim it advances, that it was the work
of an eye-witness of the events it records?   And is it
possible to harmonise its accounts with the narratives of
the Synoptists?

These are, undoubtedly, difficult questions to answer;
(ii.) **Possible** and we can only indicate here the view
solution. which appears to commend itself to a large
circle of modern scholars.   We may assume, with
tradition, that the Gospel was a relatively late production; that in fact it did not appear until towards the

close of the first century. This view is supported by the
fact that its doctrine exhibits an advance, in certain
respects, upon that of St Paul; not that it is inconsistent
with it, but mainly that, while St Paul's theology was
very largely moulded by Hebrew religious ideas, the
theology of the fourth Gospel is tempered by the thought
of the Greek world. In other words, it reflects the expansion of the Church amongst the Gentiles. Now if its
date was late, and yet the work was that of an eye-
witness, we may legitimately suppose it to have been a
collection of reminiscences, consciously seen through the
light of a profound spiritual knowledge. The view which
regards the Gospel as the work of an old man, and the
result of many years of reflection and meditation upon
the earthly life of Him whom he knew as God, has much
to commend it. It explains the omissions; for such a
writer, who would certainly have known the Synoptic
Gospels, or at least St Mark, would not have thought it
necessary to cover the same ground, but rather to supplement them with his personal recollections. It explains
the inconsistencies; for while a writer of this kind would
certainly not have manufactured events; still he would,
on the one hand, have selected only those which would
best have served to convey his teaching; and, on the
other, the passage of years might easily have conduced
to some confusion and idealisation of the pictures which
still lay in his memory. But here we may do well to
remember that even the Synoptic Gospels are no more
than fragmentary records; and that, if we had a fuller
knowledge, it might prove an easier task to harmonise
the narrative of the fourth Gospel with their own. And
again, this view explains the discourses; for it is probable
that, in the major part of them, they do not pretend to

be the actual words of Christ. It is to be noticed that there is no distinction in style between them and the author's own words; and it has been suggested that if we were to turn these discourses from the first to the third person the main difficulty would disappear; for then it would become apparent that the author was reporting, not the words but the sense of our Lord's teaching. Thus we may take it that the discourses are indeed based upon the general tenour of that teaching, and here and there contain actual words which have lingered in the author's memory; but that on the whole they represent that teaching as, after the lapse of many years, it had passed through his mind, expanded, unified, and moulded afresh. If this view can be maintained, (iii.) **Date and Authorship.** the questions of authorship and date become more simple. The Gospel appears to have been known soon after the beginning of the 2nd century. It may even have been before the Christian author of 'The Teaching of the Twelve Apostles,' about A.D. 110; though of this we can speak with no certainty. It was translated in the Old Syriac and the Old Latin versions; and it was attributed to St John, the son of Zebedee, before A.D. 170. Irenaeus records that he well remembered Polycarp, who was fond of speaking to him about St John, whose disciple Polycarp was; and Irenaeus has no hesitation in giving the fourth Gospel to St John. When we examine the Gospel itself, it appears, by the way in which it speaks of, or alludes to, St John, to claim him for its author; and when we observe that the internal evidence points to its having been written by a Jew of Palestine, who was contemporary with, and an eye-witness of, the facts reported, this is all so much additional testimony in favour of its Johannine authorship. It is possible, indeed, as some scholars affirm, that the last chapter, which is written in a different style, was added by an editor at Rome at a later date, and is comparable to the Appendix to St Mark's Gospel (Mk. xvi. 9—20); but, for the rest, there seems to be no sufficient reason why the Gospel should not be attributed to the son of Zebedee. Tradition has it that St John lived and died at Ephesus; and there, in all probability, he wrote this Gospel, some time before the Domitian persecution—say about the year A.D. 90. It is, however, necessary to add that opinion is still much divided upon the problem of the fourth Gospel.

Over the three epistles attributed to St John we need (β) 1, 2, and 3 John. spend very little time. Their similarity in style to the fourth Gospel is so strong, that a solution of the difficulties connected with the latter practically disposes of all those which can be raised in connection with the former. Thus, if we are prepared to admit that St John was the author of the Gospel, we need not hesitate to give him the epistles. The first two were probably written at the same place, and very nearly at the same time, as the Gospel; while the third may possibly date after the Domitian persecution, say A.D. 96, if verse 7 may be interpreted in this way.

The Revelation does not claim to be the work of the (γ) Revelation. Apostle, though it was very early attributed to him, and the occurrence in it of the name John lends colour to that supposition. The main difficulty, and as many think the insuperable difficulty, in the way of an Apostolic authorship lies in its language and style. This is widely different from what we are accustomed to in the Gospel and Epistles, being in places terribly ungrammatical, and throughout strongly imbued with the Hebrew idiom. Some scholars have been inclined to place the book very early, in the days of the Neronian persecution, and to account for the language by suggesting that St John had in those days but a slight acquaintance with Greek. But this does not solve the difficulty; for, on the one hand, the Greek is not that of a beginner, some of the worst offences in grammar being (as it appears) deliberate and intentional; and, on the other hand, there are certain clear indications which point to a later date, that of the Domitian persecution. This being so, the book cannot have been by the same hand as the Gospel. There remains the possibility that the book was written, if not at St John's dictation, at least under his direction, and that it embodies his own visions. But, even so, we are only left with another difficulty, that the doctrinal conceptions of the writer, his whole aim and spirit, are far removed from those of the author of the fourth Gospel. Many scholars have been inclined to see in the book a number of separate fragments of early Jewish apocalypses, which have been woven together and worked up by a Christian hand. If that is so, then at any rate the final editorial work, by one who had suffered exile at Patmos, was certainly undertaken at Ephesus during the Domitian persecution (i.e. about A.D. 95), though the component parts of the book may be ascribed to several different dates. An early Christian writer, Papias, speaks of another John, the Elder or Presbyter, who was also apparently a disciple of our Lord, and resident at Ephesus in the closing years of the century with the Apostle. It would solve many difficulties if we could confidently assign the Revelation to him.

44. The remaining books of the New Testament
Remaining Books.
(a) Acts.
we may dismiss with a few words about each in turn. The authorship and date of Acts is closely bound up with that of the third Gospel; and we have very strong grounds for assigning both works to St Luke, whose personal witness is to be found in the so-called 'we'-passages (i.e. xvi. 10—18, xx. 5—xxi. 18, xxvii. 1—xxviii. 16). A study of its style seems to prove that, unlike the historical books of the Old Testament, it is a unity, written by the same hand throughout, and not a mere editing of various materials. The latter part of the book, which is dominated by the personality of St Paul, is based upon personal knowledge, or the first-hand information of eye-witnesses; the former part, in which St Peter is the principal character, is obviously written with a less close acquaintance with the facts, though we may be sure that the author has not neglected to tap the most reliable sources of information at his disposal. Recent study has demonstrated that the author has not only woven together his material with great skill, but that he exhibited great diligence and care in the acquisition of it; so that in his book we have a most accurate and trustworthy history of the expansion of the early Church.

The epistle to the Hebrews is anonymous. The early witness to its existence generally attributes
(β) Hebrews.
it to St Paul; but various considerations seem to have led certain Christian fathers to dispute this; and, in consequence, the epistle did not at once find its way into the Canon. These difficulties may be summarised as follows. There is first of all the language and style; for the calm and deliberate progression of the argument, and the wider acquaintance with Greek,

together with a more correct standard of writing, are all
very different from what we see to be characteristic of
St Paul. Then, too, the book is rather a treatise, than a
letter in the manner of the Apostle; and, though the
author is fully in sympathy with the Pauline doctrine,
yet his treatment of his subject gives us a different point
of view to that of St Paul. We shall probably not be
wrong in reaffirming the judgment of antiquity, and
saying of it that, though it was not from the pen of
St Paul, it came from one of his disciples. The author
seems to have been a Jew, who may have been connected
with Alexandria; and the epistle, addressed perhaps to
Rome, or possibly to Caesarea or even to Alexandria,
seems to have been written before the destruction of
Jerusalem—say in A.D. 68. Several outstanding names
have been suggested in connection with its authorship,
such as Apollos and Barnabas; but perhaps that in most
favour at the present is Priscilla, who, it is urged, appears
to satisfy all the necessary conditions. She was an
intimate friend and disciple of St Paul; the fact that her
name is given, when she is mentioned in Acts, before
that of her husband, suggests that she was a remarkable
woman; she it was who instructed Apollos, the Jew of
Alexandria, and that may suggest her own connection
with that city; and the anonymity of the epistle would
be explained if it had a woman for its author. But the
matter cannot be regarded as settled.

The epistle of St James appears to be from the
pen of that James, the Lord's brother, who,
(γ) James. at Peter's departure, became the president
of the Church at Jerusalem. It seems to have been
written in Palestine, and was directed to Jewish converts
to Christianity who lived away from the Holy Land. If

indeed St James was its author we should have to place
the book very early, perhaps earlier than any other book
in the New Testament; say about A.D. 50. The reason
for this is that it appears to represent a very rudimentary
state of the organisation of the Church; to be ignorant
of St Paul's teaching about justification; and to have no
knowledge of the existence of Gentile Christianity. On
the other hand its command of the Greek language is a
very real difficulty in the way of ascribing it to St James;
and there are certain indications which would seem to
point to a late date, later even than the close of the first
century; such as its quotations from 1 Peter (unless
St Peter quoted from James), and its allusions to certain
passages in St Paul, besides a seeming contradiction of
St Paul's doctrine of justification. The arguments either
way are strong; and we may for the present leave
the authorship and the date of the epistle an open
question.

The first epistle of St Peter, on the other hand, has
every mark of being genuine. It is written
(δ) 1 Peter. in fairly good Greek; but that need raise
no great difficulty if we may recall the tradition that
St Peter had an interpreter in St Mark, and surmise that
he utilised the services of a scribe (cp. 1 Peter v. 14) in
the writing of it. The objection that the epistle is fully
in accordance with the teachings of St Paul, and that it
is written to St Paul's converts in Asia Minor, may be
met by the tradition which brings both Apostles together
in their latter years in Rome; and it is admitted that
the Babylon of the epistle, as the place of writing,
probably stands for Rome. The internal evidence, such
as the quotation of some of St Paul's epistles, the
references to persecution, and the friendly attitude which

it adopts towards the State, seems to indicate a date somewhere about 65 A.D.

The so-called second epistle of St Peter and that of St Jude, both of which were long in obtain-ing a place in the New Testament Canon, form a connected problem, owing to the fact that nearly the whole of Jude appears over again in 2 Peter. The latter appears to be the later of the two, if we may judge from the fact that its whole style is less striking than Jude, and that, in borrowing, it spoils the original. There are allusions to certain forms of heresy which proclaim the late date of both; as does also the destina-tion of both to the Christian Church at large. With regard to 2 Peter, the style and thought are widely distinct from those of 1 Peter; and the reference to the Pauline epistles shows that those were already known in a collected form at the time 2 Peter was written. We have at present no means of judging either who were the authors of these works, or where they were written; and with regard to their date, we can only conjecture that they must have been written somewhere in the first half of the second century.

45. We may leave the criticism of the New Testament with one concluding remark. Whatever may have been the dates and authorship of the various books we have had under review, and whatever may have been the history of their selection and inclusion in the Canon of Scripture; after all, the strongest evidence in their favour, and the prin-cipal claim they make to our acceptance, must always be the profound religious truth they expound; the vital spiritual experience to which they witness and which appears on the surface of their pages; and the ready

(e) Jude and 2 Peter.

The question of Inspiration.

recognition of these things, not under any compulsion but by a right judgment, which all down the ages has been awakened in the heart and mind of the Christian Church. It is such considerations as these which justify and guarantee their claim to be inspired.

BIBLIOGRAPHY.

DEISSMANN: 'Light from the Ancient East.' (Hodder and Stoughton. 2nd ed. 1911.)

MILLIGAN: 'The New Testament Documents.' (Macmillan. 1913.)

HORT: 'Introduction to the New Testament in Greek.' (Macmillan. 2nd ed. 1896.)

KENYON: 'Handbook to the Textual Criticism of the New Testament.' (Macmillan. 2nd ed. 1912.)

NESTLE: 'Introduction to the Textual Criticism of the Greek New Testament.' (Williams and Norgate. 2nd ed. 1901.)

SOUTER: 'The Text and Canon of the New Testament.' (Duckworth. 1913.)

GREGORY: 'Canon and Text of the New Testament.' (T. and T. Clark. 1907.)

WESTCOTT: 'The Canon of the New Testament.' (Macmillan. 6th ed. 1889.)

HARNACK: 'Bible Reading in the Early Church.' (Williams and Norgate. 1912.)

MOORE: 'The New Testament in the Christian Church.' (Macmillan. 1904.)

SALMON: 'Introduction to the New Testament.' (Murray. 7th ed. 1894.)

ADENEY: 'A Biblical Introduction.' Part 2, New Testament. (Methuen. 1911.)

ZAHN: 'Introduction to the New Testament.' 3 vols. (T. and T. Clark. 1909.)

MOFFATT: 'An Introduction to the Literature of the New Testament.' (T. and T. Clark. 2nd ed. 1912.)

RAMSAY: 'St Paul the Traveller and the Roman Citizen.' (Hodder and Stoughton. 7th ed. 1903.)

RAMSAY : 'Pauline and other Studies.' (Hodder and Stoughton. 1906.)

LAKE : 'The Earlier Epistles of St Paul.' (Rivingtons. 1911.)

HORT : 'Prolegomena to St Paul's Epistles to the Romans and the Ephesians.' (Macmillan. 1895.)

KENNEDY : 'The Second and the Third Epistles of St Paul to the Corinthians.' (Methuen. 1900.)

SCHWEITZER : 'Paul and his Interpreters.' (Black. 1912.)

HARNACK : 'Luke the Physician.' (Williams and Norgate. 1911.)

HARNACK : 'The Acts of the Apostles.' (Williams and Norgate. 1909.)

ROBINSON : 'The Study of the Gospels.' (Longmans, Green and Co. 1903.)

SANDAY : 'Studies in the Synoptic Problem.' (Clarendon Press. 1911.)

HAWKINS : 'Horae Synopticae.' (Clarendon Press. 2nd ed. 1909.)

BURKITT : 'The Gospel History and its Transmission.' (T. and T. Clark. 1911.)

BENNETT : 'The Life of Christ according to St Mark.' (Hodder and Stoughton. 1907.)

SANDAY : 'The Life of Christ in Recent Research.' (Clarendon Press. 1907.)

SANDAY : 'The Criticism of the Fourth Gospel.' (Clarendon Press. 1912.)

BACON : 'The Fourth Gospel in Research and Debate.' (Unwin. 1910.)

CHAPTER IV

THE RELIGIOUS AFFINITIES OF JUDAISM AND CHRISTIANITY.

1. THE growth and progress of a nation's life is The importance of environment, in general; not a matter which can be studied and understood in isolation. Similarly to the life-history of the individual, it is at every point dependent upon, and determined by, influences which reach it from the outside. The subject of historical study is always a movement and change, the course of a development and progress in one direction or another. But this development is never produced solely by the peculiar characteristics which a given race of men may be said to possess ; movement is rather, as we should say, the reaction of a nation, or individual, to a stimulus ; it is just what results when the national, or individual, qualities have been awakened by, and now respond to, the play of external forces. And what is true of the political aspect of a nation's life, holds equally good in the regions of its law, institutions, social custom, religion and literature. All these things, which are often indeed the real product of a native genius, yet exhibit a dependence, in many of their features, upon foreign influences which have been felt at different times and in different ways. We cannot really be said to understand

a thing until we can point to its origin; and thus the study of its environment is all-important.

In the present volume we are engaged in a survey of the preliminaries to Biblical study. We have passed in review the histories of the Text, Canon and Literature of the Old and New Testaments; attempting to indicate some of the special problems which call for study in each of these connections.   But our survey would not be complete, unless we were to include in it some account of the environment in which the Jewish and Christian Churches were placed, and to call attention to the sort of external influences to which they were subject, and the kind of indebtedness they may have contracted.   This is, in the main, to go behind mere literary questions to the subject-matter of Revelation itself; but the literature is, as we have seen, the record of Revelation; and, if we are to do justice to the fact of Inspiration, we cannot neglect a large part of the field of its operation.   Therefore, if we would gain a fuller understanding of the Old and New Testaments as a whole, we must read them in the light cast upon their pages by other departments of historical research; we must, that is to say, take into account the many branches of knowledge, which are found to be important aids and contributions to our critical, or historical, appreciation of the Sacred Books.

and, in particular, for Biblical study.

2.   The last century saw the birth of several new sciences, which the Biblical scholar may legitimately regard as hand-maids to his own special pursuit.   There is, for instance, the science of historical geography; for when geographical knowledge is brought into relation with historical records, it is found to afford valuable

Sources of information.

(a) Historical Geography.

explanations of the causes which led to the migrations and settlements of tribes and races of men, of their warfares and alliances; it provides reasons for the direction and character of the commercial expansion, and the international intercourse, which the history of every nationality exhibits. And, connected with these geographical studies, there is the important task of identifying, by various means, the localities and sites of ancient peoples, towns, buildings, battlefields, and

(b) Archaeo-logy. so forth. Again, there is the science of archaeology; a term which comprises the discovery and study of a great variety of objects of antiquity—inscriptions and written documents, buildings and sculptured monuments, pottery, metal and wood work, and human skeletons; all of which aid us, in different measure, to recreate the various periods and stages of culture, the civilisation and religious beliefs, of forgotten peoples; or to spell out laboriously lost chapters in the history of mighty empires of the past.

(c) The Comparative Sciences. And, once more, there are the 'comparative' sciences, as they are called; which attempt, first of all, to trace the close affinities which existed between one nation or tribe of men and its neighbours or relatives, exhibiting, so far as possible, the precise position occupied by that nation in the history of human development; and which then proceed to examine what are the qualities peculiar to it, and wherein resided its special genius. These comparative sciences branch out in all directions, to cover the whole field of human thought and activity. Physical peculiarities, language, political institutions and organisation, social customs, law, the arts and sciences, literature, morality and religion; all of them form separate fields of comparative study, and all of them contribute something, of greater or less importance, to the study of the Bible.

There are, in addition to these, other sources of information, which are, in their various degrees, of moment to the student; and these will be indicated as we proceed. It is not, however, our intention to follow out the bearings of all these sciences upon Biblical study in the present chapter; but, rather, we propose to sketch briefly the history of the contact of Judaism, and in a sense of Christianity, with other religious forces; and, thus, to suggest lines of research which the student will be able to prosecute in the authoritative books.

3. We need to feel no hesitation as to the point at Babylonia and which we should begin our sketch. The Assyria. influence of Babylonia and Assyria upon the Hebrews so far outweighs that of any other nation of antiquity, that our attention must first be directed to the land encompassed by the Euphrates and the Tigris, where these peoples had their home.

At the very early date when, by the spade of the (i.) Historical excavator, there is first disclosed to us sketch. something of the life of these primitive Semitic peoples, we discover them already emerged from a state of barbarism, and with a long history of culture lying hidden behind them. Certainly as early as 3000 B.C. their first picture writing had given place to a cuneiform script, they possessed a well defined polity in the government of their city-states, they had regulated their industrial and commercial energies, and they had established a variety of religious cults far removed from the rites of mere savages. It is now possible for us to follow the steps by which, from these remote beginnings, the great world powers emerged. For many a long century the various cities were in constant conflict with each other, only uniting occasionally to resist a common foe, or being brought together temporarily under the dominion of a successful and victorious ruler. Then, somewhere about 2000 B.C., owing to a combination of circumstances we cannot here describe, the city-state of Babylon at length effected a union of the rest under its own presidency; and Hammurabi was able to lay the foundations of the future empire. At this time the influence of Babylonian culture and civilisation was predominant throughout western Asia, extending even to Palestine and the shores of the Mediterranean, as the soldier and official followed in the steps of the travelling merchant. Some three hundred years later a foreign dynasty of kings, the Kassites, occupied the Babylonian throne, and held the reins of government during a period in which the Assyrian kingdom, perhaps an early offshoot from the Babylonian, was stirring to conscious life and independence. This synchronised with the expulsion of the Hyksos from Egypt; and the friction between Babylonia and Assyria opened the way for an advance of Egyptian arms throughout Palestine and Syria. But it is instructive to observe that, during this period of ascendancy, Egyptian officials conducted their diplomatic correspondence in the Babylonian language and cuneiform script, as witness the Tel el-Amarna letters; thus proving the deep-seated influence of Babylon in western Asia. The conflicts between the twin powers of Mesopotamia lasted over many generations, now the one being a temporary victor in the struggle, now the other; until at last the great and far-reaching conquests of Assyria, under Tiglathpileser I and Ashurnazirpal II, determined the issue in her favour.   Meanwhile Egypt, weakened in her own domestic polity, largely owing to the religious revolt of Ikhnaton, had been forced to retreat before the advancing power of the Hittites; the Philistines had established themselves upon the borders of Palestine, Assyria had been compelled to meet a new and troublesome foe in the migrating hordes of the Arameans, and the Hebrews had effected an entrance into Canaan. This brings us to about 1100 B.C.   From thenceforward we have, for the most part, a long succession of brilliant warriors in the Assyrian kings; who established the supremacy of their rule by force of arms, and by continual appeal to battle, over a period of nigh upon five hundred years, until in 606 B.C. Nineveh fell before a restored Babylonia, now ruled by a line of Chaldaean monarchs. A few years later Egypt, which had again made its power felt in Palestine, came to a final issue with Babylon and was defeated; but Babylon herself, in 536 B.C., was wrecked by the new Medo-Persian empire founded by Cyrus.   Israel had been taken captive by Sargon of Assyria in the last years of the eighth century; and Judah was led away into exile by the Chaldaean Nebuchadrezzar II in the years 597 and 586 B.C.

From this very rough sketch of the course of events, it will have become apparent that, from first to last, throughout their history the Hebrew people was subject to a very close contact with the multifarious activities, political and social, religious and economic, of their near neighbours. The legendary history of the patriarchs is cast in a country which was Babylonian territory; the invasion of Canaan by the Israelites introduced them at once to an atmosphere of Babylonian culture; the chequered history of

(ii.) **Close contact of Hebrews with Babylon.**

the northern and southern kingdoms is constantly determined by the attitude of Assyria, as they are drawn into the eddying currents of diplomacy and intrigue; commercial relations with Babylonia and Assyria were, necessarily, at all times close; and when the Jews returned to their homes under the new Persian *régime*, it was after a prolonged period of exile upon Babylonian soil. What wonder if the influence of Babylon was deep and lasting? But what, we may ask, does a comparison of Babylonian literature with our Old Testament enable us to say of that influence? How does it help our understanding? We must confine ourselves to a few points.

4. The historical books of the Hebrew Bible are obviously a series of annals or chronicles of domestic affairs, rather than of foreign relations, though these are introduced from time to time in an incidental fashion. It is also obvious that the history is in no sense a complete, or even a connected, whole; and, as we have seen, it is frequently written under the impulse of a definite point of view, and without the perception of an accurate chronological arrangement. Now the Babylonian and Assyrian historical records are in every respect a great contrast to the Hebrew books. They are, until we reach the New Babylonian empire, bald statements of fact, as a rule unadorned by picturesque touches, and bearing evidence of no ulterior motive. They are, except for mutilations, connected and full as to the matters of which they treat, such as the record of a campaign; and in point of accuracy, such matters as the complements of armies, the numbers of those slain in a battle or punished after a siege, or the amount of tribute levied, all breed in the mind of the student a feeling of confidence in their

Babylonian contributions.

(i.) Historical Records.

fidelity to fact. Up to the present the cuneiform records have given us the following list of names and events which are of direct value to the student of Old Testament history: Hazael of Damascus and Jehu 'of the land of Omri,' in an inscription of Shalmaneser III (842 B.C.); Rezon of Damascus, Menahem, Pekah and Hosea of Samaria, and Jehoahaz (Ahaz) of Judah, in inscriptions of Tiglathpileser IV (732–725 B.C.); an account of the siege and destruction of Samaria by Sargon II (722–720 B.C.); Hezekiah of Judah, and the military operations against Jerusalem by Sennacherib (701 B.C.); and Manasseh of Judah, in a writing of Esarhaddon (672 B.C.). But the references in the Hebrew books to the Assyrian marches and countermarches, and the campaigns against Syria and Egypt, are fully developed in the Assyrian records; and, while the Hebrew histories receive frequent corroboration from those sources, many obscurities in them are also cleared up by the fuller information. In a few places, however, the Hebrew supplement the Assyrian records.

But the Babylonian and Assyrian inscriptions are of direct assistance in a matter which is vital to a correct understanding of history; and that is in the chronological information they give in what are known as the Eponym lists, taken in conjunction with the Babylonian Chronicle. The absence of any era, by which the historians might have dated events, renders the Eponym lists peculiarly valuable. In these lists each king is introduced as such in the first year of his reign; and in every successive year until his death there is recorded the name of the high official of state, who, according to custom, was chosen to give his name to that year (eponym = one who gives his name).

(ii.) Chrono- logy, and the Eponym lists.

Thus the years of each reign, and the order of the kings, are accurately preserved in calendars based upon contemporary authorities; and the notes of events added to each eponymous year enable us to make an intelligent use of the detailed inscriptions, to connect up the sequence of facts with order and precision, and in some cases to date the incidents even by the month of their occurrence. It is true that the Eponym lists do not carry us behind the 9th century B.C.; but they form a stable foundation for our estimates of the chronological arrangements of preceding centuries. The event which makes it possible for us to relate this chronological system to our own, is the mention of an eclipse of the sun which took place in the month of Sivan in the eponymous year of Bur-sagale of Guzana, in the reign of Asshur-dan III; for astronomers have fixed this eclipse in the year 763 B.C. From that point, therefore, it is a simple matter to calculate forwards and backwards. Now, taking as our starting point the mention of Israelite and Judaean kings upon the Assyrian monuments, it is possible to obtain some certain and fixed dates in Hebrew history; and a further comparison of the Hebrew and Assyrian records results in a chronological scheme, certainly from the year 842 B.C. onwards, which is probably open to few objections or future modifications. Thus the cuneiform inscriptions have supplied us with invaluable material for the correct reading of Hebrew history.

But of a different character is the assistance we (iii.) Mytho-logy. derive from the Babylonian mythological texts. These are, in their originals (for in some cases the texts we possess are relatively late transcriptions), of far earlier date than the materials of Genesis. It is therefore profoundly interesting to find in them parallels to Hebrew mythology which are in some cases exceedingly close. Reference may be made to the well-known Tablets of Creation ; to the myth of Adapa, and its correspondence to the story of Paradise ; to the Gilgamesh epic, and its narrative of the Flood ; to the legend of Sargon of Agade, and its likeness to the story of Moses concealed in the ark of rushes. The differences, however, are so marked that direct borrowing is exceedingly unlikely ; and it is more probable that the Hebrew and Babylonian myths are independent developments of a common Semitic material. But, apart altogether from their main themes, these and other texts contribute much to our understanding of certain primitive ideas, which appear again and again in the Hebrew writings, about the character and constitution of the universe in which we live ; the plan of this earth, with its solid firmament of heaven, its surrounding mass of waters, and its gloomy underworld peopled with the ghosts of the dead ; the paths of the heavenly bodies—sentient spirits who influence the destinies of men ; the natures of the unseen beings, good and evil, divinities and demons, who inhabit the various forms of nature, and exercise a potent sway over human life ; the whole regions, in short, of cosmology, astrology and magic.

But it is, perhaps, in another sphere that the direct (iv.) Religious influence of Babylon can be most clearly literature. detected. The spade has reclaimed for us a whole literature of hymns and prayers and liturgies, which is of the deepest religious interest. The historical inscriptions generally strike a religious note, in so far as they represent the campaigns of the kings as being undertaken at the command of a god ; they are definitely

of a religious character when they record the building
and adorning of temples for the gods by the warrior-
monarchs.   Again, though the code of laws which has
come down to us from very early days, and which is in
many respects parallel to the so-called Mosaic ordinances,
deals nowhere with the regulation of ritual observances,
yet its provisions are given a religious basis by the fact
that Hammurabi is represented as receiving these laws
from Shamash the sun-god.   In short, these inscriptions
by themselves would be sufficient to tell us that the whole
Babylonian polity, like the Hebrew, had a religious
foundation and a religious orientation.   But in these
other texts we come nearer to the heart of the people,
and discover that they too were possessed, though in not
so high a degree as the Hebrews, of a real religious genius.
The hymns, in their outward form, present us with that
same system of parallelism which is the main feature of
Hebrew poetry; and in some passages they appear to
breathe the same spirit as that which characterises the
Hebrew Psalms.   There are texts which recall the
ideas and proverbial expressions of the Hebrew Wisdom-
literature.   In one place we have an indication of the
institution of the sabbath; in another the ritual of
sacrifice is based upon the doctrine of the substitution of
the life of an animal for that of a man; in yet another
there is found a parallel to the Hebrew scape-goat.   The
priesthood played a very important part in the life of the
community; and ritual ablutions were a means to purity,
where already a distinct conception of sin had been
formulated.   Ethical ideas were related to religious conceptions, by which both were advanced; until it came to
be seen that Divine righteousness was the reason for the
demand for human righteousness.   And it is the opinion

of some scholars that this ethical conception of the Being of God gave rise, in some quarters, to a monotheism which foreshadowed the great religious achievement of the Hebrews. In all these matters it is impossible to pronounce any verdict as to how far the Hebrews were indebted directly to Babylonia and Assyria for features which they shared in common, and how far those features were both independent and parallel developments from the same beginnings; but it would be idle to deny that the influence of Babylonia upon Israel was strong, in view of this common material and of the close political and commercial intercourse between the two peoples which persisted for many hundreds of years.

There is one other point of interest for the historical student to which we must refer before we leave Babylonia behind us. As with the Hebrews, so in Babylonia, learning was for many centuries the property of the priests. The art of writing belonged to them; they were the guardians of oral tradition and literary productions alike; and the temples of the gods were the principal national libraries, apart from that of a king like Sennacherib or Ashurbanipal. It is, accordingly, of great interest to discover that in the principal mythological texts, for instance, we are faced by the same literary problems as those which confront us in the books of the Pentateuch. Here we have the same processes of editing and revision to detect, and the same combination of various sources into a literary whole to unravel. This is instructive as a proof of the literary habits of the Semitic peoples, and as an additional corroboration of the validity of the critical methods applied by scholars to the books of the Old Testament Canon.

5. The civilisation of the Nile valley is of more
Egypt. His- profound antiquity than that of the Meso-
torical sketch. potamian plains. We have, in Egypt as
in Babylonia, evidence of a lengthy period which stands
on the threshold of history proper, during which the
country was divided between a number of petty principalities, or city-states, in constant conflict with each
other, until one was able to assume a position of
paramount authority, and so to weave the disconnected
units into a single kingdom. But this process appears
to have reached its completion at least a thousand years
earlier in Egypt than in Babylonia ; and Egypt had
already been for many centuries a strong, united and
flourishing state, remarkable alike for its commercial
development, architectural and artistic achievements,
social organisation and religious feeling, before ever
Hammurabi came to establish the Babylonian civilisation upon a permanent basis. It is clear that at a very
early date trading relations were established between
Egypt and Syria ; and even in the 19th century B.C. we
hear of Sesostris III despatching a military expedition
against certain Syrian states. But it is not until some
two hundred years later that the events transpired which
led to the rise of an Egyptian empire in the near east.

(a) The With the decline and fall of what is known
Hyksos. as the Middle Kingdom, there followed a
period of domestic confusion and anarchy, during which
the country lay prone to the invasion and dominance
of a foreign power. This power was that of a Semitic
state which had recently been consolidated in Syria and
Palestine, and which had the seat of its government at
Kadesh on the Orontes ; and it is usually known as the
Hyksos. The Hyksos appear to have ruled Egypt for

upwards of a hundred years; and it was doubtless during this period that certain Bedouin tribes of the Arabian desert, known later as the Hebrews, effected a settlement in the Delta. It may even be that one such tribe rose to a position of temporary supremacy in the land ; for a monument of the time gives Jacob-her (or perhaps Jacob-el) as the name of an otherwise unknown Pharaoh. Under Ahmose I, the founder of the first Egyptian empire, a new impetus was given to the national life, and slowly the Hyksos were expelled from the borders of Egypt. The subsequent organisation of the various departments of social and political life bears a distinct resemblance to the work said to have been accomplished, in the Hebrew legend, by Joseph as vizier of the Pharaoh; and it is probable that a popular tradition, later combined with some elements of the well-known story of ' Anpu and Bata,' may have been the foundation of the tale in Genesis. Succeeding kings, not content to have freed their country from foreign rule, pushed their advantage against their retreating enemies ; and during the next hundred years Syrian campaigns form the most important feature in the reigns of the several Egyptian monarchs. And at length Thutmose III, the greatest soldier Egypt ever produced, succeeded in crushing the last vestige of the Hyksos power, while at the same time he extended his sway throughout Syria to the banks of the Euphrates.

The Asiatic empire of the Pharaohs was, in the main, a military sway exercised over conquered peoples, who could only be held in subjection so long as Egyptian arms continued to be energetic and repressive. Egyptian history has nothing to show of the Assyrian policy, which sought to weld

(b) **Egypt in Syria.**

the various peoples into a single homogeneous state, by constant deportations of the inhabitants to different parts of the empire, and by a spread of cultural influences. Thus, so soon as Egypt lost her power to impress her will upon the conquered, and both soldiers and official governors were withdrawn, her very memory was quickly blotted out. And this, in point of fact, happened before the next hundred years had passed.

Recent excavations, prosecuted mainly at Senjirli, in (c) The the extreme north of Syria, and at Boghaz-Hittites. keui, within the great semi-circle formed by the Halys river of Asia Minor, have given us much interesting information about the great Hittite empire, the very existence of which was, until the last few years, still in the region of myth. It was the steady advance of the Hittites southwards into Syria, which now began to menace, and ultimately broke, the Asiatic dominion of Egypt. At the same time a people known as the (d) The Khabiri, a group of Bedouin nomads who Khabiri. probably included Aramean and Hebrew elements, were pressing upon the borders of Palestine and Syria from the south and east. The letters discovered at Tel el-Amarna are, to a large extent, a diplomatic correspondence between the Egyptian sovereigns and their Syrian representatives, on the one hand, and, on the other, the monarchs of Babylonia, Assyria and other nations. These tell a tale of impotence and political folly on the part of Egypt, at a time when Ikhnaton was devoting all his energies to religious innovation; and they, together with tablets discovered at Boghaz-keui, which all use the cuneiform script, are valuable, as we have already seen, for the evidence they give us of the wide diffusion of Babylonian culture, even during the period of Egypt's supremacy in Syria.

From time to time, during the second Egyptian empire, renewed efforts were made to gain a hold upon western Asia, by Seti I, Ramses II, Merneptah and Ramses III ; but they proved ineffectual, and that for various reasons. Egypt never possessed the spirit and genius of a military power, and her great efforts under the first empire had completely exhausted her energies. Moreover, the religious movements had produced an economic depression and political restiveness which constantly weakened her resources. And when a new (*e*) The wave of Philistine immigration from the Philistines. north, which forced the remnants of the Hittites into Palestine where the Hebrews subsequently found them, began to occupy the length of the Mediterranean coast-line, Egypt had no longer any power to cope with the situation. It is in an inscription relating (*f*) Israel and to the Palestinian conquests of Merneptah the Exodus. that the name of Israel first occurs ; and then it is as a people or nation, the result of a process of tribal cohesion. There is no reference in any of the extant Egyptian records to an extensive exodus of Hebrews from the Delta ; but a Jacob-tribe may well have been reduced, in those times, to a condition of serfdom, and utilised for the building of such places as Pithom and Ramses, in the reign of Ramses II ; and this may well have been a reason for their escape, perhaps in the reign of Seti II (about 1200 B.C.), and for the migration which led them to their own kinsmen in the Sinaitic peninsula. The condition of the Canaanites, as the indigenous peoples of Palestine may be called, at the time of the influx of the Hebrews, their culture, religion and degree of civilisation, may be determined in some measure by the results of the excavations which have been proceeding for some years past upon the mounds marking the sites of the ancient towns. The story of their conflict with the Philistines and other peoples is given in their own recorded traditions.

Some two hundred and fifty years after the exodus Sheshonk I, the founder of a Libyan dynasty, *(g) Egypt and the Hebrew monarchy.* controlled the destinies of Egypt; and possibly it was he who established a family connection with King Solomon. Certainly at a later date, after the partition of the Hebrew kingdom, he invaded Palestine, spoiled Jerusalem, and possessed himself, amongst other localities, of 'the field of Abram.' From that time forward Egypt was forced to reckon with the expanding power of Assyria, which now began to contest with her the sovereign rights in Palestine and Syria. Egyptian troops came for the first time face to face with Assyria at the battle of Qarqar in 854 B.C., where Shalmaneser II was the victor. But the Pharaohs were intent upon avoiding, if possible, a direct trial of arms, and rather preferred to enlist the services of Judah and other intermediate principalities, who should, as buffer-states, bear the brunt of the Assyrian's warlike operations. It was against this foolish intrigue with Egypt that Isaiah was never tired of inveighing; and time and again Judah was made to suffer for her short-sighted policy. It was during the period of Ethiopian supremacy that Egypt was entered by Assyrian armies, first under Esarhaddon, and then under Ashurbanipal; and it was to the latter that Thebes, the ancient and glorious mistress of Egypt, eventually capitulated in 661 B.C.

With the fall of the Ethiopian power, on the one hand, and the extinction, on the other, of Assyria by the New Babylonian kingdom, Egypt was free to effect the last restoration of her ancient glory; a renaissance which spread over a period of a century and a quarter. It was then that Necho made a final bid for the control of Syria, defeating Josiah at Megiddo, only however to be himself finally crushed by Babylon at Carchemish in 605 B.C. When Jerusalem fell before Nebuchadrezzar, and the people of Judah were deported to Babylon, many Jews escaped to Egypt and settled there; and recently a number of Aramaic papyri have been discovered at Elephantinê, which reveal something of the life of the descendants of these refugees about a hundred years later. Egypt herself did not actually fall to Babylon; but she was entered by Cambyses in 525 B.C., and became a province of the Medo-Persian empire in that year.

(h) Egypt and Hebrew dispersion.

6. The Hebrew writings frequently betray an intimate knowledge of Egypt, her social customs, her trade interests, her domestic history, and so forth; but at no point do they lead us to suppose that the influence of Egypt upon the moral and religious life of Israel was ever very profound. Egyptian literature comprises a large range of historical texts, the annals of kings in the conduct of their wars and in the administration of their kingdom, and other like things, inscribed or painted mainly upon the walls of temples and tombs. Much of the literature of Egypt is contained in papyrus rolls, which the extreme dryness of the atmosphere has preserved to us through thousands of years. There are books of proverbial wisdom, folk-songs, mythical relations, and stories

Egyptian contributions.
(i.) Literature.

composed for entertainment; but no code of laws is
extant. The religious literature is, as a whole, impressed
with what we must regard as the most prominent and
impressive feature of the Egyptian religion; and that
is its intense belief in a future life. The mortuary texts
contain long and elaborate directions, which were intended
to guide and conduct the soul in its voyaging through
the gloomy underworld to the fields of immortal bliss.
These are mingled with fragments of mythical lore; and
gradually there is incorporated into them more and more
of those magical formulae which were directed towards
preserving the soul from the incredible perils which
awaited it in the next life. The so-called 'Book of
the Dead,' the great religious writing of the Egyptians,
which was the outgrowth of centuries and was often
revised, is almost entirely a magical work. There have
come down to us certain religious poems, which already
exhibit the beginnings of that parallel construction which
is characteristic of Semitic poetry; and the most remarkable of these is Ikhnaton's 'Hymn to Aton,' which
possesses some features in common with Psalm 104.

(ii.) Theology. Egyptian theology cannot be studied as a
single connected scheme; but is rather an
incoherent mass of separate beliefs which arose at different
times and in different localities. At one time one god
was in the ascendancy, at another a different one, according as the political power of his chief seat of worship
waxed or waned. Ptah, the artificer-god of Memphis,
during the first empire became a divine supreme intelligence, whose creative 'word' may have been the germ
of the conception later developed by Greek and Christian
philosophy. Re, the sun-god, and Amon who practically
displaced him, were always the chief gods of the Egyptians;

and the introduction by Ikhnaton of the god Aton was a refinement of solar worship which promulgated an idea in advance of his age—that of a single and universal god, spiritual in nature and beneficent in his works. And throughout the whole period of Egyptian history the worship of Osiris appears to have been the dominant cult amongst the masses of the people; a cult which, more than any other perhaps, was associated with ethical and religious features of age-long value. For Osiris was the divine saviour of men, who enabled them to assume the righteousness which alone could pass them through the ordeal of judgment and admit them to immortal life; and through him there was inspired in men's hearts, on the one hand a sense of the guilt of sin, and on the other a desire for that divine communion which ensures the future bliss. It is perhaps remarkable that the Osiris myth should have had no distinct influence upon the religious conceptions of the Hebrews. But, if this is so, at least we seem to see some connection between the earlier stages of the Hebrew Messianic doctrine, and the Egyptian idea of a coming age of destruction and misery, in the midst of which will appear a Saviour who is the 'shepherd of his people.' Viewing the matter as a whole, we shall probably be right in saying that whereas the links connecting Babylonian religion with the Hebrew are many and strong, those which connect the Egyptian with it are few and obscure, notwithstanding the close historical association between the peoples, spread over many centuries.

7. We must now, for a short space, revert to the beginnings of Hebrew national history, and consider the influences brought to bear upon the people in their infancy, in their new found home in

The Hebrews in Canaan.

Palestine. The land was inhabited by a number of independent tribes of Semitic race, who are collectively known in the Old Testament as Canaanites. The coast-lands were in the possession of the Philistines, a non-Semitic people whose native home may have been Cyprus and the southern regions of Asia Minor. Further to the north were the powerful seafaring Phoenicians, who were also Semites. To the east of them were located the Aramean tribes who were even then coalescing into principalities, such as Damascus, which at a later date were to play an important part in the fortunes of the Hebrew nation. More closely related to the invaders were an inner circle of petty kingdoms on the south and east of Canaan, Ammon, Moab and Edom, who, in the fore-front of the Bedouin migration, had already found for themselves settled seats. And, more loosely organised, there was yet an outer fringe of tribes, in a transitional stage between the nomadic life of the desert, and the pastoral life of Palestine, Midianites, Amalekites and Ishmaelites, with such smaller tribal divisions as the Kenites and the Jerahmeelites. With all these tribes the Hebrews had very close affinities, in race, language, religious and social customs; but whereas the Hebrews were only just emerging from a condition of primitive barbarism, the nearer these other peoples were situated to the Mediterranean littoral, the more settled was the condition of their life and the more highly organised was their civilisation. A flood of light has been thrown, as we have observed, upon the degrees of culture to be found in and about Canaan at this period by recent archaeological discovery; some of the more important evidence comprising inscriptions of Phoenician and other origins, chief amongst which is the famous Moabite stone of King Mesha, the contemporary of Ahab and Jehoram of Israel. And, where contemporary evidence is lacking, a great many blank spaces may be filled in by a study of the manners and customs of the Arabian tribes of the present day, who exhibit a phase of culture remarkably similar to that we read of in the Hebrew books.

8. Yielding, perhaps, to the pressure behind them of the South-Arabian Sabean civilisation, the Hebrews appear to have pressed in upon Canaan in successive waves of immigration which lasted over a long period. This period of conquest synchronised with a change of habit, whereby the desert marauders became, in course of time, an agricultural populace. Superior in force of arms to those by whom they were opposed, they had everything to learn from the indigenous peoples they overcame. Possessed of no genius for anything but religion, they displayed an astonishing aptitude for assimilating all the culture which the higher civilisation could impart. The invasion was not that of a united people, but rather of scattered tribes ; it was therefore not concentrated upon any one field, but dispersed over a large tract of country. From this it followed that the Canaanite tribes, though vanquished in detail, were not dispossessed ; they were neither driven out nor obliterated, but continued to dwell side by side with their conquerors, with whom inter-marriage produced a mixture of blood and an interchange of ideas and customs. It could not fail, therefore, that the Hebrew religion should become permeated by Canaanite influences. The tradition of an original twelve tribes is probably a reading back into a dim past of the organising state-craft of Solomon ; but, however this

Hebrew invasion of Canaan.

may be, the original bodies were not united, and the work of amalgamation was long and arduous. First there came the period of the judges—the various efforts, only local and frequently contemporary, on the part of the new settlers to break the bonds of Moabite or Philistine rule, to which the Canaanites had probably been accustomed. In one place this produced a temporary kingship, in the person of Gideon, which gave a precedent for the subsequent action of Samuel. But it was not until the royal power, in the hands of Saul and David, had compelled the allegiance of all the scattered Hebrew tribes, that a national life became for the first time possible. And it would have been during that long transitional stage that alien religious ideas impressed themselves most strongly and indelibly upon the Hebrew consciousness.

9. The Canaanites shared in common a devotion
Hebrew conception of God. to the male and female divinities, Baal and Ashtoreth; the Philistines had their various city gods, such as Dagon of Ashdod or Baalzebub of Ekron; Moab and Ammon (and probably Edom) had advanced to the conception of a single national god, in Chemosh and Milcom. So Yahweh of the Hebrews, from being a tribal deity who moved about with his people, became first a local god, when he was often identified with the Canaanite Baal who had preceded him, and then a national god, similar to Milcom of Ammon. At each stage in this development the Hebrew theology and ritual of worship was similar to, and probably received somewhat of, the other cults in the midst of which it took form. At one time Yahweh had his portable shrine secreted in a Bedouin tent; at another he was worshipped at high places, marked out as sacred

by the upright stone, wooden pillar (asherah), or grove; and again his dwelling was established at a central temple, with its great altar of sacrifice.

10. Humanly speaking, we may say that it was an accident which singled out the Hebrew divinity as God's mode of revealing Himself to men; so that, before the Christian era, all that was most noble and most profound in man's knowledge of the Eternal and Almighty, was veiled under the name of Yahweh. There was no reason in the nature of things that we can see, why any other of the gods of antiquity should not have been selected as the means of this communication of the truth. But it was so that the Hebrews alone, amongst all primitive peoples, possessed in a peculiar degree that religious genius which enabled them to travel furthest and highest in the conception of God, and of His relation to men. It was so, that they alone developed in its higher ranges the spirit of prophecy, through which the communication of truth was made. And for this reason the study of the nature and functions of the prophet, and the history of Hebrew prophecy, is one of the most important and valuable in the whole range of Biblical research.

Revelation of God through Yahweh.

11. The foregoing reflection enables us to return a satisfactory answer to two questions which appear to have exercised the minds of some of the early Christian fathers. The one was whether it was possible to identify the Christian God with the Hebrew Yahweh; and to this we must reply that, in so far as the Hebrews and Jews came to clothe their conception of Yahweh with the attributes of the God whom Christians worship, we may; but the further we go back in the history of the Hebrew religion, the more

Yahweh and the God of Christians.

Yahweh sinks to the level of the gods of the heathen, and the less able are we to affirm of him that he is the true God.

12. The other question relates to the degree of

apprehension of the true God other peoples

God revealed
Himself to
others, but
especially to
Hebrews.

or individuals, who had no knowledge of Yahweh, may be said to have possessed; the worshippers of Marduk or Amon, for instance, or certain of the Greek philosophers. And the answer we are surely justified in returning is, that God has never limited His revelation of Himself, and that under many and diverse systems of religion and philosophy men have been inspired to grasp some of the deepest truths of the spiritual life; so that in all we are bound to discover certain elements which are vital to all religion. Moreover, the Hebrew religion itself appears to have developed partly by borrowing from other sources factors which contributed greatly to its own lofty conceptions. But, on the other hand, in no other nation do we discover so strong a faculty for grasping, assimilating and advancing God's self-revelation to men; and for this reason the Hebrew religion became, ethically and spiritually, by far the noblest religious force, by far the truest theological creed, of pre-Christian days.

13. It was in the latter part of the eighth century

that Samaria fell; and with its downfall

Passing of
Israel, and rise
of Samaritans.

Israel, as a nation, was blotted out of existence. Large numbers of the people were deported to other towns of the Assyrian empire, where they were gradually assimilated to the manners and customs and beliefs of their captors, and thus inevitably deprived of all national identity. Others fled and took refuge in Egypt and elsewhere, and thus yielded themselves to the same disintegrating conditions; while the victorious monarch poured into the territories of the northern kingdom a heterogeneous mass of alien colonists, who by intermarriage came to mingle their blood with that of the remnant of the Israelites ; with the result that, from the mixture of races was produced the Samaritan people, at whose hands the post-exilic Jews were fated to suffer so much of hostility and persecution. This inevitably led to the further degradation of a religion, which already, previous to the conquest, exhibited the signs of deterioration. Yahweh, though still worshipped by a section of the people, became again but a local Baal, one of the many gods acknowledged by a servile and decadent population ; and he was again worshipped with rites similar to those of other deities, though still retaining certain of the characteristics of the ancient Hebrew cult. Thus it was that Israel passed out of the main current of formative religious impulse ; and with the southern kingdom of Judah remained the task of carrying high the torch of revealed truth.

14. The period of the exile is probably the most important in the whole range of Old Testament history ; and yet it is a period regarding which we have very little direct testimony, and which we are compelled to reconstruct in the main from the historical allusions of the prophetical writings. The historical writings desert us here, though they resume again with the era of reconstruction in Judaea after the exile. But Josephus, the later Jewish historian, at this point begins to provide us with valuable information ; and this is supplemented by the extant Babylonian inscriptions. At a later period, during the Persian and Greek rules, there are again inscriptions which come to our assistance ; while the writings of the

Extra-Biblical historical authorities.

Greek historians enable us to obtain a very adequate grasp of the historical background to the picture of Jewish development. And here again the late prophetical writings, psalms and other pieces of Jewish literature become of great importance to us.

15. In three separate detachments, in 597, in 586 when the temple was destroyed, and again in 581 B.C., the Judaean Hebrews, to the extent of nearly half their numbers, were led captive to Babylonia. It is necessary to grasp the fact that the period of the exile was in reality the commencement of those Jewish dispersions, which at a later time were to play so prominent a *rôle* in the religious history of the people. It is true that the catastrophe, which spelt the ruin of all that the Hebrews most treasured,—the extinction of the royal dynasty, the demolition of the temple and the cessation of its sacrificial rites, the sacking and destruction of the sacred city, and the annihilation of an independent nationality,— was for the time being quite overwhelming. But by that means other countries and peoples became permeated with Jewish ideas and moral and religious influences; and out of the ruin there arose, in course of time, a compact state which definitely embodied a religious principle, and attracted the attention of the world by reason of its lofty ideal. During the exile there took place a mighty transformation, whereby the remnants of a semi-pagan principality emerged as a religious community, and the Jewish Church was born.

In Judaea Nebuchadrezzar left a fairly numerous peasant population, governed by a few nobles. Left to themselves they suffered grievously from the treachery of one of

The Exilic period, and the beginning of Dispersions.

(i.) The Judaean Remnant.

their own number, and from the constant persecution of their enemies. They fell to a condition of extreme poverty and wretchedness, and heathen religious practices gained ground amongst them. But no colonists from Babylon were settled in Judaea, and the native inhabitants were able to retain their racial identity; they were fortified from time to time by some who had fled before the Babylonian armies, and now chose to settle again in their own homes; and the worship of Yahweh was still continued at the local shrines, and sacrifice offered at an altar erected on the site of the ruined temple. Thus the returning exiles came back to find a condition of affairs not essentially different from that of pre-exilic days.

But, on the other hand, large numbers of Judaeans fled from their homes at the beginning of the exilic period to find refuge in Egypt, (ii.) The Egyptian Dispersion. where they received a welcome from the reigning Pharaoh, Hophra, who was inclined to encourage the settlement of foreigners in his dominions. Carrying the prophet Jeremiah with them, they made their home in the Delta regions, where they probably joined hands with the previous emigrants from Israel. They threw themselves, there, into all kinds of commercial pursuits, and mingled freely with the Greek settlers who were now a conspicuous feature in the population. Later, they penetrated southwards to upper Egypt; and in the next century they appear to have built themselves a temple at Elephantinê, where they continued to practise the rites of their religion. At the same time many of them gave themselves over to heathen cults, and appear to have revived the worship of an old Semitic divinity, 'the Queen of Heaven,' who may be identified with Ishtar and Aphrodite.

The task of religious development seems to have
(iii.) The
Babylonian
Dispersion. been given, almost exclusively, to the exiles
in Babylonia. This may be accounted for
by a combination of circumstances. In the
first place, at least in the case of the first deportation, it
was only the best of the Judaeans, intellectually and
spiritually, prophets and priests, princes and nobles, who
were carried away by Nebuchadrezzar. From this richness of quality and capacity there was produced a long
line of very remarkable men, prophets and priests and
scribes, who fanned the spark of hope, kept alive the
religious faith of the exiles, developed plans for the future
reconstruction of their state, and undertook a vast labour
of literary composition, historical, moral and spiritual.
But, in addition to this, the exiles were not scattered, as
was the custom with the Assyrian monarchs in dealing
with their captives, and as they dealt with Israel. On
the contrary they appear to have been allowed to settle
in a single tract of country, by the Chebar canal, east-
wards of Babylon and not far from Nippur. They were
free to trade, to govern themselves by their own laws, to
practise their own religion, and to advance themselves to
official posts under the government. Thus they were not
swamped by intercourse with the native populations, nor
reduced to slavery, nor compelled to the adoption of the
Babylonian divinities; but were in a position to maintain
a certain measure of independence, and to organise themselves into a free and regulated community. It is true
that only a minority took advantage of the opportunity
to return to Judaea, afforded them by the decree of
Cyrus; for many had doubtless formed commercial
connections which rendered the return inexpedient to
them. But the more religious spirits amongst them had

long cherished the hope of return ; and when their dream was realised, they were able to take up the reins of self-government in Judaea because of the freedom they had enjoyed in Babylonia.

16. The national ruin they had experienced, and the exile they suffered, were the predisposing causes of the great religious advance made by the Jews during this period. The exiles, as was natural, dwelt fondly and regretfully upon the glories of the past ; and this led them to a study of history. In this study they became acutely conscious of the important part the prophets had played in their national life, of how they had foolishly neglected to profit by God's repeated warnings, and of how events had subsequently proved the prophets to have been in the right ; and this drove them to lend a willing ear to the living words of inspired men in the present. Enforced absence from the home-land, Yahweh's own country, im-plied an alienation of the people from their God ; the law was in abeyance, the festivals had ceased, no sacrifice could be offered, the central shrine of their worship was destroyed. But this all conspired to emphasise the sense of sin and the duty of penitence ; it created a desire for some means of atonement, whereby a divine communion might be restored. And this desire was, in its turn, the fertile soil which nurtured the growth of some of the higher characteristics of the Jewish religion. The exile saw the beginnings laid of a splendid and brilliant literary activity ; and the products of this activity wit-ness to the rapid and sure progress of religious faith and religious organisation. With the conception of a single God, went the belief in the universal character, and the righteousness, of that God. The rise of an ecclesiastical

The causes of religious development.

community implied a government by the priesthood. The grasp of the relation in which His people stood to God produced a realisation of the necessity of fasting, of the observance of the sabbath, of purification and the distinction between clean and unclean, and of the study and development of the Law. The lack of a temple encouraged the growth of the synagogue, which became a means both of instruction and of devotion, in prayer and in psalmody. Hopes fixed upon the future probably sowed the first seeds of apocalyptic and eschatological thought. Thus, if the exile was indeed the nursery of so much that was essential to the Jewish religion, it could not but be that these varied factors in theology and ritual observance were, in large measure, moulded by influences encountered for the first time, or most powerfully then, in and during the period of captivity.

17. But the exilic period marks only the opening of a great constructive era, continued right through the days of Persian domination. It was in 538 B.C. that Cyrus entered Babylon, and the Medo-Persian empire was established in the greatest city of antiquity. The conqueror initiated a new policy in dealing with subject races; for, instead of terrorising them into submission and obliterating their national characters and aspirations, he conceived the idea of attaching them to his throne and person by kindly treatment, and by conferring upon them the blessings of orderly and sympathetic government. An extant inscription tells us that he gave a general permission, not to Jews only but to all captive peoples, to return to their native homes, and to carry with them, where it was still possible, the goods of which they had been dispossessed. The hopes and gratitude

The Persian period, and its stimulus to religious activity.

which his policy stirred in Jewish hearts led the exiles
to herald Cyrus as Messiah, and to attribute to him a
devotion to the service of Yahweh. It is improbable
that the contingent of exiles who took advantage of
the imperial decree to return and rebuild their temple
in 537 B.C. was at all numerous. It is not likely that
Sheshbazzar, the newly appointed governor, took with
him more than his personal retinue. Certainly in 520,
when Zerubbabel was governor and Joshua high-priest,
the population of Judaea was still sunk in poverty and
ignorance; and it was only then, in response to the
encouragements of the prophets, that the rebuilding of
the temple was enterprised. Thus the inception of the
political and religious restoration which was to follow
was practically the achievement of those who had never
left their homes to dwell in the land of exile. But the
improvement in the conditions of life and religion which
they effected, under the kindly auspices of Persia,
gradually tempted others to return, both from Babylonia
and from Egypt; and the combined culture and patriotic
feeling which they brought with them undoubtedly helped
forward the movement, and laid it upon a strong and
permanent basis. The temple was finished in 516 B.C.;
and with that there was again inaugurated the sacrificial
system at a central shrine.

18. But from that date, for seventy years Jewish
history in Palestine is a blank; and when,
in 445 B.C. with the coming of Nehemiah,
the veil is once more lifted, we perceive that the period
had not been characterised by much of religious or
social progress. The disturbed state of the country, the
indigence of the Jewish community, the hostility of
their neighbours—Samaritans, Edomites, Ammonites and

The reforms of
Nehemiah.

Arabians,—the lack of culture and the absence of any master mind amongst them, all had tended to moral laxity and spiritual deterioration. The real renaissance of Judaism commenced with Nehemiah, who came from Susa, with the authority of Artaxerxes I, to rebuild the walls of Jerusalem. With him came a large train of patriots, all inspired with a zeal for the Law as it had been developed in the far land of exile. Both on that occasion, and with greater vigour and effectiveness on his subsequent visit in 432 B.C., Nehemiah set to work to publish the Law, and to gain the adhesion of the people to its operation in the re-established Jewish state. With extraordinary courage, determination and statesmanship, he overcame all opposition, in the face of armed hostility from without and treachery from within. Jerusalem was rebuilt, the temple worship restored, and all kinds of social reforms were realised. It was in pursuance of this programme of reformation that he introduced that policy of exclusiveness, which was ever after characteristic of Judaism. Marriage with the heathen was severely prohibited; the Samaritans, who had hitherto regarded the temple at Jerusalem as their own, were peremptorily expelled from a religious partnership with the Jews; and proselytism was discouraged.

19. Doubtless the picture of religious purity which

The work of Ezra.

Judaea now presented proved attractive to many of those dwelling in the foreign dispersions, who were zealous for an unrestricted liberty in the practice of the rites of their faith. Thus, when the priestly scribe, Ezra, set out from Babylon somewhere towards the close of the 5th century (the date is not yet precisely determined), he was accompanied by far the largest body of exiles who ever returned in a single migration. It was Ezra's function to build upon the foundations Nehemiah had laid, and to carry his reforms to a fitting conclusion. Upon the Deuteronomic Law was now superimposed the Priestly Code, with its elaborate system of ritual observance. From henceforth the State was dominated by the Church, as the priesthood gradually absorbed all the functions of civil government. And undoubtedly the speedy progress in social affairs which accompanied this religious development was in large part due to the fact that now, for the first time, the returning exiles numbered in their ranks men of substance, as well as of culture, whose wealth gave an added support to the common weal. These were the happiest, as they were the most constructive, days of Jewish national life; but they were soon to be ended by a period of gloom and persecution. Tempted, by the growing weakness of Persian rule, to make an effort to gain political independence, the Jews threw in their lot with a number of rebel peoples, and suffered severely for their temerity. Artaxerxes Ochus crushed the rebellion with a heavy hand, pillaged Jerusalem, desecrated the temple, and transported a number of the people in bonds to the southern shores of the Caspian sea. This was in 346 B.C.; and fifteen years later the Persian empire lay in the dust.

20. For the most part the Persian despotism had Persian proved genial and paternal; and for this contributions. reason the Jews showed themselves ready to respond to the influences, social and intellectual, which reached them in and from Persia. Moreover there was something, morally and spiritually, of kinship between Judaism and the religion of Persia, Zoroastrianism, which would have attracted the attention of the cultured Jew. Zoroaster, like Moses, was said to have proclaimed the precepts of his religion as revealed by the one God; and that religion, like the Hebrew, was distinctly ethical. Zoroastrianism, again, like Judaism was organised as an ecclesiastical polity, in which the priesthood was the dominant factor; it also had a similar institution to the synagogue for purposes of public worship; and it also laid down a similar distinction of clean and unclean. It is therefore not a matter of astonishment to find that Persian religious ideas exercised a strong influence in the formation of the Jewish beliefs and practices. As with the Babylonian, it is not easy, or perhaps possible, to say how far this Persian influence was direct; how far, that is to say, the Persian beliefs simply operated to develop what was already implicit in Judaism, and how far Judaism actually borrowed from Zoroastrianism. But, if in nothing else, Judaism appears to be indebted to Persia for much in her later doctrines of the resurrection, with a future apportionment of rewards and punishments, and of spirits, the good and evil angels who congregate about the persons of Yahweh and of Satan,—that personification of evil, who recalls the dualism of Zoroaster in the twin beings Ormuzd and Ahriman.

21. In the year 332 B.C. Alexander the Great conquered Syria, together with the provinces of Palestine; and in the following year his hand closed upon the last vestiges of the domination of Persia. In Judaea the fear of Persian reprisals withheld the welcome which would otherwise have greeted his coming; but so soon as it was perceived that the old order had passed, the Jewish state readily gave itself to the enjoyment of the liberty and culture

The Greek period, and the beginnings of Hellenism.

which Greek rule brought in its train. One of the greatest works of the conqueror was the building of the city which perpetuated his name in the Egyptian delta; and it was not long before Alexandria possessed a large Jewish quarter. But, in addition to this, Alexander's statesmanship was exhibited in the large number of Greek towns which sprung up under his initiative throughout Syria and Palestine, populated to a large extent by Greek colonists, and becoming the centres of the Greek culture which, with the Greek language, gradually filtered throughout the conquered provinces. His ambition was to make the whole world Greek; and in a great measure he succeeded in doing so. To many of the Jews, cramped in their age-long isolation and rigid exclusiveness, the new ideas thus imported were as the breath of a new life; and, yielding easily to the attraction, Hellenic customs, language and culture quickly became a fashion.

After the death of Alexander in 323 B.C. his various generals, or satraps, plunged into a long conflict, as the result of their individual assumption of independence or supreme authority. The fortunes of war gave Egypt to Ptolemy, while Antigonus extended his sway from Asia Minor to Persia. Thus Palestine, as lying between these two territories, became a bone of contention, and the battle-field of foreign armies; and the Jews were again made to suffer, as their Hebrew forefathers had suffered from the conflicting claims of Egypt and Assyria. With the death of Antigonus, Ptolemy became master of Palestine; and his successors were able to retain their hold upon the country against Seleucus and his descendants, who were lords of Syria, for near upon a

(i.) Ptolemaic rule.

hundred years. All this while, however, the Jews were rather courted than oppressed by the rival contestants; and the conditions of life in both Alexandria and Antioch were so happy as to attract many to leave their homes and voluntarily to become exiles. Ptolemy Philadelphus is reported to have extended his patronage, and made gifts, to the temple at Jerusalem; and it was during his reign, and perhaps by his encouragement, that the Greek translation of the Hebrew Scriptures was commenced.

In the person of Antiochus the Great the Ptolemies eventually found a foeman of superior quality; and in 198 B.C. Palestine passed under Seleucid sway. It was at this time that large numbers of Jews were drafted, not unwillingly, to colonise certain provinces of Asia Minor, Phrygia and Lydia, where they are discovered with their synagogues in New Testament times. In the same year was fought the battle of Magnesia, which signalised the beginning of the extension of Roman power in the east. There followed a few years of peace; until the accession of Antiochus Epiphanes in 176 B.C. heralded the opening of one of the most terrible chapters in Jewish history.

(ii.) Seleucid rule.

Antiochus was possessed of Alexander's zeal for Hellenising the Asiatic kingdoms; but his zeal outran his discretion, and he did not hesitate to resort to the most brutal and unscrupulous means to forward the ends he had in view. During the Greek period the advance of Hellenic culture had made such great and rapid strides that the Jewish religion was in great danger of being entirely blotted out; and this process Antiochus determined to hasten to a conclusion. But

(iii.) The persecutions of Antiochus Epiphanes, and the rise of religious parties.

over against this extreme liberalism there had gradually
asserted itself an intense conservatism, which was inspired by an almost fanatical zeal for the Law and the
customs of the fathers. Within Judaism itself had
grown up two opposite tendencies, which were rapidly
becoming consolidated in a division of the nation. On
the one hand there was the love of foreign ideas and
customs, which produced free-thought and religious
apostasy; on the other a revival of the ancient standards,
which rapidly crystallised into a narrow bigotry and
a bitter hatred of all outside influences. The former
tendency was espoused by the aristocratic party, the
forerunners of the later Sadducees, and even captured
the higher ranks of the priesthood. The latter was the
faith of the minority, the poor and oppressed, who were
known as the Chasidim or Puritans, from whom sprung
the later Pharisees. The period which saw the rise of
these party, or sectarian, divisions, also witnessed the
growth of the Sanhedrin, which was later to act as a
curb upon the autocracy of the high-priests. Of the
high-priests little valuable information has come down
to us. Some were undoubtedly men of saintly lives,
such as Simeon II, who flourished in the reign of
Antiochus the Great, and who was known as 'the Just';
while others, like certain of the mediaeval Popes, were
men of infamous character. Moreover, during this period,
we can trace the rise of apocalyptic idealism, on the one
hand, and, on the other, that practical wisdom in which
the Scribes sought to apply the genius of the Law to the
problems of daily life; both of which tendencies produced
large additions to the mass of Jewish literature. And,
side by side with these, as a result of that Greek
philosophy which was now permeating the cultured

thought of Palestine, we have an outburst of religious scepticism, which finds expression in the words of Agur, and in the book known as Ecclesiastes.

This is not the place to recount the incidents which led to the ferocious attempt, on the part of Antiochus, to end Judaism; the apostasy of Jason, the treachery of Menelaus, the sacking of Jerusalem, the erection in the Temple courts of an altar to Zeus, the blood-thirsty persecution of the faithful who with magnificent devotion gave their lives for their religion, the revolt of the aged priest Mattathias with his five sons, the astonishing military aptitude of Judas and his extraordinary victories over successive Syrian armies, and the capture of Jerusalem and dedication of the purified temple in 165 B.C. The whole narrative has come down to us in 1 Maccabees, supplemented by 2 Maccabees and the relation of Josephus. But with the Dedication it may be said that Greek rule in Palestine was already broken, and a new era had commenced.

22. This era is known as the Maccabaean (Maccabaeus, the Hammerer, being a name popularly given to Judas), or Hasmonaean (since Judas' grandfather was one Hasmon). It began as a revolt against persecution, inspired by religious motives; its sole aim was to restore again the worship of Yahweh in all its purity, and it was supported by the whole force of the Chasidim. But inevitably it could not end there; and it gradually assumed the proportions of a political movement, an attempt to win a national independence, and to set up a self-governed state free from the intervention of foreign rule, at a time when Syria was being hard pressed by

the advancing tide of Roman dominion, and torn by
internal dissensions. The struggle against Syria was
renewed in 164 B.C., when Antiochus Epiphanes died;
and it continued with scarcely any intermission until
143 B.C., when the sovereign independence of the Jewish
state was at length recognised by Syria and Rome alike.
The history of these twenty and more years is intricate,
and the fortunes of the patriot Jews exhibit constant
alternations of triumph and reverse. It is a period
characterised by intrigue and cruel reprisals; a period in
which the Hellenistic party gain the upper hand when-
ever they can capture the ear and aid of Syria; and the
orthodox, on the other hand, when the feuds between the
rival claimants to the Syrian throne direct the attention
and energies of their foes to their domestic affairs, and
Judaea is left for the time to work out her own salvation.
The three Maccabaean brothers, Judas the soldier,
Jonathan the skilful diplomatist, and Simon the constructive statesman, stand out prominently as the founders
of the Jewish state; and all three are justly famed for
their unselfish devotion to their religion and country.
Judas fell in battle in the year 161 B.C.; Jonathan, who
after an interval succeeded the Hellenising Alcimus as
high-priest in 153, was brutally murdered by his Syrian
captor in 143 B.C.; and in 135 Simon was assassinated by
his own son-in-law, Ptolemy. But Simon was worthily
succeeded by his son John Hyrcanus, who during a long
reign of thirty years built solidly upon the foundations
laid by his predecessors. At his death, however, the
religious policy of the Maccabees was reversed, and
Hellenising influences were once more allowed to
dominate the land. Moreover, under his two sons,
Aristobulus and Alexander Jannaeus, the latter's wife

Alexandra, and his son Aristobulus II, the process of disintegration set in which was ultimately to lay Palestine at the feet of Rome. This was due in great measure to the bitterness of sectarian strife, encouraged by the sympathies of the successive sovereigns, which made anything like orderly government an impossibility.

23. The Hasmonaean rulers were not content to free their own country from foreign rule. They realised that if they were to build up a stable and permanent state it must be by the acquisition of fresh territory. Consequently, by a succession of aggressive wars, they gradually brought other lands and peoples under their dominion. In 130 B.C. the temple on Mount Gerizim was destroyed, and in 106 Samaria itself was demolished and its territory added to that of Judaea. In 129 B.C. the Idumaeans, the descendants of the older Edomites, were conquered, and forcibly compelled to adopt the religion of Judaism. And in 105 a portion of Iturea, including the later Galilee, was absorbed and its population similarly converted. The Hasmonaean rulers gathered the whole powers of government into their own hands. In all but name they were kings; and the title was withheld only because the Messianic expectation demanded that the dignity should be reserved for the Prophet when he should appear. They were also high-priests; and both offices, united in the one person, were held to be heritable in the Hasmonaean family. But their autocratic powers were limited by the Sanhedrin, which was the political machine of the two great parties in the state alternately, the Sadducees and the Pharisees.

Hasmonaean rule.

24. During this period we may watch a tendency towards religious conservatism in the people at large, who, under the guidance of the Pharisees, grew less sympathetic towards the Sadducean Hellenistic spirit. But while a greater rigidity in doctrine took form in Judaea, there was a strong development in the Jewish dispersions, particularly that of Alexandria, in the direction of a liberalism which owed much to Hellenic thought and culture. There we observe the growth of a broad and enlightened type of Judaism, very far removed from the shallow religious apostasy of the Hellenistic party in Palestine. The social exclusiveness of the Jew, and the tenacity with which he held to his doctrines, far more than the peculiarity of his tenets, earned him an evil reputation in the Hellenic world; and this defamation of character produced in him a zeal for self-defence, which in turn created a large apologetic literature, the object being to exhibit the reasonableness of the Jewish faith. Now this literature, of which the Sibylline Oracles is one of the most prominent members, gives signs of a wide acquaintance with the masterpieces of Greek writing; and thus shows how Judaism itself was infected with the culture of the west. But Alexandrine Judaism more especially set itself the particular task of effecting a reconciliation between philosophy and revelation; for it anticipated a great triumph for the Jewish religion if once it could be shown that the noble speculations of the Greek philosophers were not alien to the truth as God had declared it, in history and experience. From Aristobulus (circ. 170 B.C.), fragments of whose work are preserved by Eusebius, to Philo and beyond, this great task was enterprised; and allied to it was an allegorical method of interpreting the Hebrew Scriptures, which was obviously capable of lending additional support to this theory. The book of Wisdom exhibits a doctrinal development, which was bound to be the result of a fusion of Greek thought with Hebrew; and such a development was a very real preparation of the ground for the seed of the Gospel.

25. It seems that it was also in this period that there originated the monastic brotherhood known as the Essenes, who combined a refinement of Pharisaic principles and practice with something in the nature of sun-worship, which may have had a Persian lineage, but which, far more probably, was due to an infusion of Greek philosophical ideas. Thus Essenism may be another witness to the currency of Hellenic thought amongst the Jews.

The Essenes.

26. Reference has already been made to the building of the Samaritan temple on Gerizim, and to the existence of a Jewish temple at Elephantinê in upper Egypt; and for this reason we may, in passing, draw attention to yet another temple, that of Leontopolis, which was founded in the year 160 B.C. The reasons which led Onias IV to take this unusual course may have been various; the usurpation of the Hellenisers, Jason and Menelaus, whom he could not consider legitimate high-priests; the desolation of the temple at Jerusalem; the comfort and encouragement of orthodoxy. But this temple continued in existence until 73 A.D.; and, though it was defended by an appeal to Is. xix. 19, it is probable that this course was a result, as it was certainly a cause, of a growing estrangement between the liberal Jews of Alexandria and the rigidly orthodox Jews of Palestine.

Temple at Leontopolis.

27. In the year 66 B.C. the Roman arms, under
The Roman period. Pompey, had advanced to the overthrow of
Mithridates, king of Pontus, and Tigranes
of Armenia; and the attention of the future mistress
of the world was now seriously drawn to the broils
which continuously vexed the Jewish state. Three years
later Pompey was in Damascus, where he received a
deputation from the Pharisees, who were then politically
in disfavour; and this determined him to take action.
Aristobulus resisted, but ineffectually. Jerusalem was
taken, the temple was profaned, and Palestine became
a Roman province. Galilee and Syria were merged in
the government of Syria; Judaea was placed under the
rule of an ethnarch, Hyrcanus, who was also appointed
high-priest; and the Jewish people entered upon the last
stage of its national career, again as a subject race.
Alexander Jannaeus had, early in his reign, appointed
a certain Antipater to the governorship of Idumaea;
and this man was succeeded by his son who bore the
same name. The son had been largely instrumental
in gaining for Hyrcanus the position of authority to
which he was appointed, when his brother Aristobulus
was carried prisoner to Rome. Antipater now became
Hyrcanus' vizier in Judaea; and so great was the
ascendancy he obtained, by the arts of diplomacy and
intrigue, over that weak representative of the Maccabaean
line and his supporters, that he was able to place his
own sons in positions of virtual sovereignty; Phasael
in Jerusalem, and Herod in Galilee. Thenceforward
Palestine was rent by the dynasty broils between the
last of the Hasmonaeans, Aristobulus II and his two
sons Alexander and Antigonus, and the new Idumaean
family which came to be known as the Herodian.

28. It was not until the year 40 B.C. that Herod
obtained a full recognition from Rome of
Herodian rule.
his kingship; and it still required three
years of campaigning in Palestine before he could make
his authority felt, and could enter upon his reign as
master of the whole country from Idumaea to Galilee,
and east as well as west of the Jordan. He ruled indeed
as the vassal of Rome; but so skilfully did he assume
the *rôle* of loyalty, while changing his allegiance always
to the victorious side in Roman domestic affairs, whether
it were Pompey or Antony or Octavian, that he was left
in a position of practical independence.

At no time subsequent to the Roman acquisition of
Jewish territory did the unhappy land know peace. The
people who lived in the memory of the glorious stroke
for freedom accomplished by the Maccabaean fraternity,
and in whose veins ran the blood of an intense patriotism,
could never reconcile themselves, despite the advice of
the Pharisaic party, to the yoke of a foreign overlordship; and they were restive and fractious, ever anxious
for an occasion to revolt. Moreover, the Idumaean line
was, in their eyes, a hateful usurpation; and the Herods
were always unsympathetic to a populace in whose
breast was growing the Messianic hope of a king of
the Davidic line. And, in addition to this, the cruel
despotism and oppression of an absolutism which could
brook no rivals, and which sought to exterminate all
opposition, had its fruits in lawlessness and brigandage,
the inevitable results of bad government.

29. Herod the Great was a pagan at heart; and
though he had the good sense to respect, in
Hellenising policy.
some measure, the principles and worship
of Judaism, he frankly set himself to change the character

and spirit of the people by the encouragement of
Hellenistic feeling. To the treachery and brutality
of a savage he allied the culture and the splendour
of western civilisation. He introduced and supported
heathen cults; he patronised gladiatorial games and
theatrical spectacles, which were exhibited in the very
shadow of the temple; he lavished untold sums of
money on great building enterprises, including his own
palace and the castle of Antonia at Jerusalem, fortresses
throughout the country, the town and harbour of Caesarea,
which now became to all intents and purposes the capital
of Palestine, and lastly, as a tardy bid for popularity,
the temple itself; and he did much to develop the
agricultural and commercial interests of the land. But
his was a reign of terror, intensified by suspicion and
intrigue, ambition and ferocity, and a host of domestic
infelicities. The Sanhedrin was robbed of all power;
the Sadducees and Pharisees were practically expelled
from political life, and driven to seek refuge in theological
strifes; the nobility and people were hopelessly alienated;
and the Herodian court party, which now came into existence, was the measure of the distance which separated the
Herods from the people they were called upon to govern.

30. On the death of Herod the Great, in the year
4 B.C., by his will the country was partitioned
out to three of his sons. To Archelaus was
given Judaea, Samaria and Idumaea; to
Herod Antipas, Galilee and Perea; and to Philip, several
small provinces to the north and east of the lake of
Galilee. The whole was subject to the supervision of
the Roman legate of Syria. The rule of Archelaus
was so thoroughly despicable that in the year 6 A.D. he
was banished, and his territory was handed over to a

The last phase of Jewish national life.

Roman procurator. Herod Antipas, though an adherent of Hellenism and, as such, unacceptable to his subjects, was a favourite of Tiberius; and so anxious was he to stand well with Rome that he was careful not to abuse his power; and he succeeded in maintaining his position until 39 A.D. Philip, whose rule was said to be just and beneficent, but who certainly was spared the irksome duty of dealing with a Jewish population, died in 34 A.D. Three years later Agrippa, grandson to Herod the Great and brother to Herodias, who was the wife successively of Philip and Herod Antipas, was appointed by Caligula to succeed Philip; and in 39 A.D. there was given to him, in addition, the territories of Herod Antipas. In 41, he had so succeeded in ingratiating himself with the emperor Claudius, that Samaria and Judaea were also added to his dominions; and once more Palestine was in the hands of a single native ruler. But when he died in 44 A.D. the whole country reverted to the governorship of a Roman procurator. It is unnecessary to follow any further the evil fortunes of the Jewish state, or to trace the pitiful history of those last years, during which the people were driven to madness by the incurable depravity of a long succession of incapable procurators, and in which they were torn by the strife of factions; the Zealots thirsting for war at all costs, the Pharisees resisting to the utmost the incredible folly of their opponents. The end came with the Roman invasion of Palestine under Vespasian in 67, and the fall of Jerusalem, after a five months' siege, to Titus in the year 70 A.D.

31. From that time the Jews ceased to be a nation; and the only organisation they were to know in the future was ecclesiastical. Judaism became wholly a dispersion,

The later Jewish Church.

without any central shrine to focus the devotion and hope of the scattered people. Jamnia was the scene indeed of a religious revival, under the leadership of the Scribes and Pharisees; but the ritual of sacrifice was perforce discontinued; the Synagogue now took the place of the Temple; and the Priest was succeeded by the Rabbi. Living scattered throughout the nations, refusing to become fused with the peoples amongst whom they dwelt; citizens of the empire, privileged to practise their religion and exclusive habits with an unaccustomed freedom; the dispersed Jews became now a proselytising church, devoted to the religious salvation of humanity, and inspired by the golden dream of a Messiah who would come and restore to them all, and more than all, that they had lost.

32. This last period added nothing directly to our Biblical literature; but it was the period

The literary products of this period.

in which Jesus of Nazareth lived and died, and Christianity took its rise. Thus it is most important for the student of the New Testament; for it provides the historical background and setting, without a knowledge of which we cannot hope to understand the genius of that religion which was destined to dominate the world. Before we go on to examine the influences which played, from its inception, upon the doctrines of Christianity, we must glance at two products of this later Judaism which are, in different ways, of

(i.) Apocalyptic works.

great importance for our purpose. The one is the large range of apocalyptic literature, of which we have already seen the beginnings, and of which so much has come down to us. This literature exhibits, primarily, the reaction of Judaism in its contact with the heathen world. Starting from the hope of a purely temporal kingdom, theocratically administered in the person of Messiah and characterised by a righteous adherence to the Law; the hard facts of experience drove the writers to look to a vindication of their religious faith, and a righting of the injustices from which they suffered, in the far future, and under conditions essentially different from those of a temporal kingdom. They began to see visions of a different age and another world; in which the Messiah should be superhuman, if not Divine, the kingdom a Church of the redeemed, and its members the souls of the righteous. The hope of a resurrection to immortal life dawned upon these inspired seers; and the future was pictured by them under a great variety of images, and in ever changing forms.

The second product of the Judaism of this period (ii.) Rabbinical literature. is the vast range of Rabbinical literature. This was as yet only in a traditional form, in the making, and handed from scribe to scribe by word of mouth; for it was not codified until several generations were passed, nor written down for centuries to come. But indubitably a great part of this literature dates back to these times; and, while it exhibits the tendency to an intense legalism which later became the dominant characteristic of the Jewish spirit, it serves to throw much light upon the period in which Christianity took form. This literature is based upon the canonical authority of the Hebrew Scriptures. The Mosaic Law is binding in its force, but only partial in its scope. It was the function of the scribe to expand and develop this Law until it should cover every department of life, and meet every conceivable circumstance. The scribal decisions were treasured, and orally passed on as themselves possessing equal force with the Law itself; they were 'halacha,' or binding rules. These decisions were collected and codified in no less than sixty separate tractates, which were known as the Mishna. But in time this naturally became antiquated; and scribal activity developed a huge commentary or interpretation of the Mishna, which was itself arranged and codified as the Gemara. The whole of this material constitutes the Talmud, which exists in two different forms, the Palestinian and the Babylonian. But, in addition to the commentaries on the law, the scribes busied themselves with allegorical interpretations of Scripture, and speculations upon all things in earth and in heaven, which, while having no binding force, were conceived to be material for entertainment and edification, or 'haggada,' and therefore carefully preserved and handed down orally. This sort of matter is the main constituent of what are known as the Midrashim. And, further, when Hebrew had become a dead language, it was necessary to translate the passages of Scripture read in the synagogues into Aramaic; and these translations, which are frequently paraphrases, are contained in yet another branch of Rabbinical literature known as the Targums, of which the principal are those of Jonathan and Onkelos. Just as the Roman rule in Palestine led to the development of apocalyptic thought, so the wave of Hellenism under the Herods produced a legalistic revolt, which led to the growth of this Rabbinical literature.

33. The cradle of Christianity was the Jewish Church. The ethical and religious doctrines of our Lord do indeed exhibit many traits which bear a more or less close resemblance to those of other religious teachers—even

Indebtedness of Christianity to the Old Testament, and to Judaic thought.

perhaps to those embodied in writings so far afield as
the Buddhist. But, if borrowing there has been, these
things had already filtered through the minds of the
Jewish Rabbis; and Jesus Himself only reproduces
ideas which were already current in His Jewish environment. To allow that He was indebted to a great
extent to the Hebrew Scriptures is only to recognise
what is apparent on the surface of the Gospel narrative,
and to perceive that Jesus regarded those Scriptures as
a true record of God's self-revelation to men. And to
admit the possibility that He was further indebted to
other teachers, apocalyptic and rabbinical, in no way
minimises the originality and supreme value of the
revelation which was entrusted to Him. The co-
ordination of all that was most true in
what the moral insight of other teachers
had led them to expound, and the weaving
of all this into a single, perfectly balanced and harmonious
type of character; the insistence that the moral life,
rightly understood, is freedom and not law, and that
this freedom is to be realised through sacrifice, inspired
by love; the emphasis laid upon man's spiritual nature
and capacities, in which alone life itself consists, and
which bases character upon the communion of the soul
with God; and, above all, the supremely adequate presentation of this teaching in the features of His own
character and life:—herein we may find the originality
of Jesus and the genius of Christianity. But, if we would
correctly estimate the true force of His doctrine, we must
not divorce it from its historical associations, or neglect
to observe where He adopts and develops the ideas of
others, giving them new point or applying them with
freshness of treatment; and where He unconditionally

(i.) **Measure
of the origin-
ality of Jesus.**

splits with the past, and announces Himself in opposition to His predecessors. In general, we will notice that there is much in the spirit and aspirations of the apocalyptic writings which He endorses and makes His own ; while the tendencies of Rabbinism rather act as a foil to His teaching, in contrast and opposition to which He is best able to expound His own doctrines with power and life.

There can be no reasonable doubt that, in the earliest days of the Christian Church, the outlook (ii.) Hebraic character of of its members was strictly Jewish, just as early Church. their environment and manner of life was Palestinian. The Hebrew Scriptures, the temple sacrifices, the synagogue services,—these were sufficient for the small company of Jews who felt that in Jesus they had discovered their Messiah. And when the earliest community was driven far afield by persecution, it was to take refuge in the Jewish dispersions, which were less narrow in their outlook, but where, nevertheless, the same conditions of life awaited them. A religious sect, a fraction of the Jewish Church, whose ideal was that of a regenerated Judaism with the hope of Messiah fulfilled,—in such a fashion did the Christian Church take its rise. The (iii.) Expansion of Church leads to transvaluation— Hebrew thought in Hellenic dress. proselytising energies of the Jewish dispersions, perhaps, first turned the thoughts of Christians to a wider field ; this, and the circumstance of their rejection by the Jewish communities to whom the Messiahship of Jesus was unacceptable, led them to embrace the whole Gentile world in the field of their operations. It is to the genius and statesmanship of St Paul, the Roman citizen, and to his friend St Luke, that we must attribute the first clear perception of the universal nature of Jesus' work, whereby the Jewish Messiah becomes the World-Saviour; and in their writings we may trace the small beginnings of that long process, in the course of which Christianity was to take on a western dress, to clothe itself in the language and thought of the Hellenic world, and to model its organisation after the pattern set by the forms of Roman imperial administration. But the complete shedding of its original oriental character was not accomplished until several generations had passed. When Christians first began to assemble for worship in their own private houses or elsewhere, their services were similar to those of the Jewish synagogue; and the organisation of the separate Christian communities, in the towns of the western world, was at first a reproduction of the methods of the Jewish dispersions, whose life was centred in the synagogue with its controlling elders and ministers. Even the Christian prophet was but a revival of the order which had disappeared in Israel.

It is true that the epistles of St Paul abound in allusions to other than Jewish customs and ideas, which cannot be understood apart from some knowledge of the Greek and Roman world in which the Apostle moved. An interesting example of this is to be found in the repeated use he makes of the condition and status of the slave, the position of the debtor, or the upbringing of the child. It is also true that he makes considerable use of the terms of Greek philosophy in the exposition of his doctrines. But this was in itself unavoidable; and a close examination shows there is little trace to be found in his writings of the conceptions for which those terms stood in their original context. The flooding of Christian doctrine by Greek philosophy, in the form which it acquired in

(a) Hebraism of St Paul.

Alexandria, was to come later; but of St Paul we may confidently affirm that, if the expression was Greek, the thought was still definitely Hebrew in its main features.

(*b*) **Hellenism of St John.** The Johannine writings, as we should expect, exhibit a change in this respect. In them we seem to come into closer contact with Greek philosophical ideas; but, even so, perhaps we should be right in saying that it is a Greek philosophy which has already permeated the Jewish world, the philosophy which the school of the Alexandrine Jew, Philo, had endeavoured to reconcile with Hebrew revelation. A conflict with heathen ideas, such as the deification and worship of the imperial master of the Roman world, may often have played an important part in developing the disciples' grasp upon the fundamental doctrines of Christianity; just as the conflict with Judaism, which produced a plentiful crop of heretical sects in the early Church, also strengthened and purified the Christian's understanding. and interpretation of the Gospel message. But this is not the same as to say that Christianity owed those elements in its teaching to external sources, from which it borrowed wholesale. The fundamentals

(*c*) **Little trace of direct influence from other sources.** of Christian teaching are the product of its own inner spirit; and the indebtedness of Christianity is almost wholly confined to Judaism. Even the Babylonian and Persian apocalyptic imagery of the book of the Revelation was already domiciled in Palestine before it fell into the hands of the Christian writer. That heathen religions, and especially those known as the Mysteries, came to have an influence upon Christianity, especially on its ritual and sacramental side; and that Christianity, in contact with these religions, was led to a larger and deeper grasp

of the implications of its own doctrine and life, so that
it was able to feel an affinity with what was best in the
Gentile world;—all this is probably most true. But it
belongs to a period which lies beyond the range of the
New Testament; and, as a whole, our canonical literature
exhibits few traces of such influences.

34. Thus, while a study of the heathen world in
the first century of our era is of first-rate
importance for our understanding of the
beginnings of Christian history,—the rapid
spread of the new religion, the means to its organisation,
the setting of its life, the moral and religious problems
which faced it, and so forth,—it is not to the heathen
world that we shall go for the genesis of Christian
doctrine. For Christianity was, in a measure, continuous
with Judaism, and was evolved out of it; and, apart
from the revelation of Jesus Himself, it is to the Hebrew
Scriptures we must go, to the Wisdom literature and
the extra-canonical apocalyptic books, to discover the
sources of its inspiration. The history of Judaism itself
reveals an indebtedness now to this source, now to that,
in the long course during which it gradually arrived at
the sublime conceptions which informed its religious life.
The unique revelation of Jesus Christ was the glorious
edifice erected upon the foundations so laboriously laid.
It answered to the note of expectancy which characterises
the whole of the Hebrew Scriptures; it was the fulfilment
to which the Jewish dispensation was a preparation.
The revelation which had previously come in divers
manners and at different times, in the desert, in exile,
or in the home-country, sometimes from Canaanite or
Babylonian, sometimes from Persian or Hellenic sources,
was now crowned with a manifestation of God's truth,

Continuity of Christianity with Judaism.

complete and final, in the Person of Jesus Christ. And it is that final revelation which we study in the pages of the New Testament, as the product and the outcome, in some measure, of what had gone before, and as interpreted for us by the inspired vision of those who truly knew Christ, if not after the flesh, yet more adequately in the Spirit.

BIBLIOGRAPHY.

A. *Geography and Archaeology.*

G. A. SMITH : 'Historical Geography of the Holy Land.' (Hodder and Stoughton. 9th ed. 1902.)

G. A. SMITH : 'Jerusalem. The Topography, Economics, and History from the earliest times to A.D. 70.' 2 vols. (Hodder and Stoughton. 1908.)

SANDAY : 'Sacred Sites of the Gospels.' (Clarendon Press. 1906.)

DRIVER : 'Modern Research as illustrating the Bible.' (Frowde. 1909.)

RAMSAY : 'The Cities of St Paul; their Influence on his life and thought.' (Hodder and Stoughton. 1907.)

B. *Hebrew and Jewish History and Religion.*

KITTEL : 'A History of the Hebrews.' 2 vols. (Williams and Norgate. 1895.)

SAYCE : 'The early History of the Hebrews.' (Rivingtons. 2nd ed. 1899.)

SAYCE : 'Patriarchal Palestine.' (S.P.C.K. 1912.)

KENT : 'A History of the Hebrew People.' 2 vols. (Smith, Elder. 12th ed. 1913.)

KENT and RIGGS : 'A History of the Jewish People.' 2 vols. (Smith, Elder. 1912.)

SCHÜRER : 'A History of the Jewish People in the time of Jesus Christ.' 5 vols. (T. and T. Clark. 1908.)

CHEYNE : 'Jewish Religious Life after the Exile.' (Putnam. 1898.)

BUDDE : 'Religion of Israel to the Exile.' (Putnam. 1899.)

MONTEFIORE : 'The Origin and Growth of Religion, as illustrated by the Religion of the Ancient Hebrews.' Hibbert Lectures. 1892. (Williams and Norgate. 3rd ed. 1897.)

ROBERTSON SMITH: 'The Religion of the Semites.' (Black. 1901.)

MARTI: 'The Religion of the Old Testament.' (Williams and Norgate. 1907.)

OESTERLEY and BOX: 'The Religion and Worship of the Synagogue.' (Pitman. 2nd ed. 1911.)

CHARLES: 'Eschatology; Hebrew, Jewish and Christian.' (Black. 2nd ed. 1913.)

C. *Babylonian and Assyrian History and Religion.*

GOODSPEED: 'History of the Babylonians and Assyrians.' (Smith, Elder. 1903.)

ROGERS: 'History of Babylonia and Assyria.' 2 vols. (Eaton and Mains. 4th ed. 1910.)

JASTROW: 'Religion of Babylonia and Assyria.' (Ginn. 1898.)

ROGERS: 'Religion of Babylonia and Assyria.' (Luzac. 1908.)

JASTROW: 'Religious Belief in Babylonia and Assyria.' (Putnam. 1911).

JEREMIAS: 'The Old Testament in the Light of the Ancient East.' 2 vols. (Williams and Norgate. 1911.)

ROGERS: 'Cuneiform Parallels to the Old Testament.' (Frowde. 1913.)

D. *Egyptian History and Religion.*

BREASTED: 'A History of Egypt.' (Hodder and Stoughton. 1906.)

BREASTED: 'A History of the Ancient Egyptians.' (Smith, Elder. 1912.)

BUDGE: 'A History of Egypt.' 8 vols. (Kegan Paul. 1902.)

PETRIE: 'A History of Egypt.' 3 vols. (Methuen. 1897.)

MAHAFFY: 'History of Egypt under the Ptolemaic Dynasty.' (Methuen. 1899.)

MILNE: 'History of Egypt under Roman Rule.' (Methuen. 1898.)

WIEDEMANN: 'Religion of the Ancient Egyptians.' (Grevel. 1897.)

ERMAN: 'A Handbook of Egyptian Religion.' (Constable. 1907.)

BUDGE: 'The Book of the Dead.' 3 vols. (Kegan Paul. 1901.)

SAYCE: 'The Religion of Ancient Egypt.' (T. and T. Clark. 2nd ed. 1913.)

236 BIBLIOGRAPHY

E. *Hittites.*

MESSERSCHMIDT : 'The Hittites.' (Nutt. 1903.)

SAYCE : 'The Hittites.' (R.T.S. 5th ed. 1910.)

F. *Persian History and Religion.*

HASTINGS : 'Dictionary of the Bible.'
CHEYNE and BLACK : ' Encyclopædia Biblica.' } Articles on Persia and Zoroastrianism.

MOULTON : 'Early Zoroastrianism.' Hibbert Lectures. (Williams and Norgate. 1913.)

JACKSON : 'The Religion of Persia.' (Promised by Ginn and Co.)

CUMONT : 'The Mysteries of Mithra.' (Kegan Paul. 1903.)

CUMONT : 'The Oriental Religions in Roman Paganism.' (Kegan Paul. 1911.)

G. *Greek Religion.*

HARRISON : ' Prolegomena to the study of Greek Religion.' (Cambridge University Press. 2nd ed. 1908.)

FARNELL : 'The Higher Aspects of Greek Religion.' (Williams and Norgate. 1912.)

ADAM : 'The Religious Teachers of Greece.' (T. and T. Clark. 1908.)

LIVINGSTONE : 'The Greek Genius and its Meaning to us.' (Clarendon Press. 1912.)

JEVONS : ' Introduction to the History of Religion.' (Methuen. 1896.)

RAMSAY : ' Religion of Greece and Asia Minor'; in Hastings' 'Dict. of Bible': extra vol.

H. *Roman Religion.*

FOWLER : 'The Religious Experience of the Roman People.' (Macmillan. 1911.)

I. *Christianity and its Environment.*

HORT : 'Judaistic Christianity.' (Macmillan. 1894.)

RAMSAY : 'The Church in the Roman Empire.' (Hodder and Stoughton. 8th ed. 1904.)

BIGG : ' The Church's Task under the Roman Empire.' (Clarendon Press. 1905.)

GWATKIN : 'The Knowledge of God, and its Historical Development.' 2 vols. (T. and T. Clark. 1906.)

CLEMEN : 'Primitive Christianity, and its Non-Jewish Sources.' (T. and T. Clark. 1912.)

A TABLE OF THE EXTANT HEBREW, JEWISH AND CHRISTIAN LITERATURES, CHRONOLOGICALLY ARRANGED, UP TO ABOUT 180 A.D.

N.B. For the most part the dates of the completed books, rather than of their several parts, are given.

It must be remembered that, in the majority of cases, the dates can only be approximately given.

The canonical books of the Old and New Testaments are printed in ordinary type, the others in italics.

B.C.

750.	Amos.
850—750.	*Elohist Document.* (E.)
730.	Hosea.
690.	Micah.
900—650.	*Jehovist Document.* (J.)
625.	Zephaniah.
610.	Nahum.
650—600.	[*Combination of* J *and* E.]
600—580.	Lamentations.
586.	Habakkuk.
570.	Ezekiel.
570.	Obadiah.
520.	Haggai.
520—518.	Zechariah i—viii.
680(?)—500.	*Deuteronomist.* (D.)
600—500.	Isaiah i—xxxv.
580—500.	Jeremiah.
500.	Job.
500.	Ruth.
530—450.	*Deutero-Isaiah.*
500—450.	[*Combination of* D *with* JE.]
450.	'Malachi.'

B.C.

580(?)—400.	Priestly Code. (P.)
450—400.	Trito-Isaiah.
390(?).	[*Combination of* P *with* JED.]
370.	Joel.
370(?).	*The Samaritan Pentateuch.*
280.	Jonah.
600(?)—250.	Proverbs. [The highest date is that of the earliest collection.]
250.	Zechariah ix—xiv.
300—250.	Chronicles—Ezra—Nehemiah.
200.	Ecclesiastes.
200.	Song of Songs.
200.	Esther.
165.	Daniel.
150.	*Tobit.*
150.	*Baruch* i—iii. 8.
150.	*Letter of Aristeas.*
140.	1 *Esdras.*
450—135(?).	Psalms. [The highest date is that of the earliest known collection.]
250—132.	*The Septuagint.*
180—130.	*Ecclesiasticus.*
120.	2 *Maccabees.*
140—110.	*Book of Jubilees.*
109—107.	*Testaments of the Twelve Patriarchs.*
100.	*Judith.*
100.	*Additions to book of Esther.*
90.	1 *Maccabees.*
100—80.	*Prayer of Azaria.*
100—80.	*Song of the Three Children.*
100—80.	*Bel and the Dragon.*
100—80.	*History of Susanna.*
175—64.	*Book of Enoch.*
100—50.	*Wisdom of Solomon.*
50.	3 *Maccabees.*
50.	*Prayer of Manasses.*
63—48.	*Psalms of Solomon.*
18—8(?).	*Zadokite Work.*

A.D.

1—50.	*Book of Secrets of Enoch.*
7—30.	*Assumption of Moses.*
30.	4 *Maccabees.*
50.	Q (=Sayings of Jesus ?).
50(?).	James.
53.	1 Thessalonians.
54.	2 Thessalonians.
56.	Galatians.
56.	1 Corinthians.
57.	2 Corinthians x—xii.
57.	2 Corinthians i—ix.
57.	Romans.
62.	Colossians.
62.	Philemon.
62.	Ephesians.
62.	Philippians.
64.	1 Timothy.
64.	Titus.
65.	2 Timothy.
65.	Mark.
65.	1 Peter.
68.	Hebrews.
70—72.	Luke.
74.	Acts.
75—80.	Matthew.
70—80.	*Apocalypse of Baruch.*
70—80.	*Baruch* iii. 9—v.
90.	Fourth Gospel.
91.	1 John.
91.	2 John.
95.	Revelation.
96.	3 John.
50—100.	*Ascension of Isaiah.*
80—100.	*Epistle of Jeremiah.* (=*Baruch* vi.)
95.	*Clement of Rome:* 1 *Corinthians.*
110.	*Teaching of the Twelve Apostles.*
110.	*The Epistles of Ignatius.*
112.	*Epistle of Polycarp.*

A.D.

120.	*Apology of Quadratus.*
160 (B.C.)—130.	*Sibylline Oracles.*
90—130.	*Epistle of Barnabas.*
140(?).	2 Peter.
140(?).	*Gospel of Peter.*
140.	*2 Corinthians, attributed to Clement.*
140.	*Epistle to Diognetus.*
140.	*Apology of Aristides.*
145(?).	Jude.
145.	*Apocalypse of Peter.*
150.	*'Shepherd' of Hermas.*
150.	*Protevangelium of James.*
70—150(?).	*Odes of Solomon.*
150.	*Justin's Apology.*
158.	*Justin's Dialogue with Trypho.*
160.	*Clementine Homilies.*
170.	*Acts of Paul and Thekla.*
170.	*Tatian's Diatessaron.*
176.	*Epistle from Lyons and Vienne.*
177.	*Apology of Athenagoras.*
180.	*Irenaeus, 'Against Heretics.'*
70—270.	*2 Esdras.*

For EU product safety concerns, contact us at Calle de José Abascal, 56–1°, 28003 Madrid, Spain or eugpsr@cambridge.org.

www.ingramcontent.com/pod-product-compliance
Ingram Content Group UK Ltd.
Pitfield, Milton Keynes, MK11 3LW, UK
UKHW012330130625
459647UK00009B/191